Basic Biology Questions
for Standard Grade

Also from Stanley Thornes (Publishers) Ltd

BIOLOGY QUIZZES AND PUZZLES   G. Curtis

A FIRST BIOLOGY COURSE   P. T. Bunyan

LIFE SCIENCE – Groundwork in Biology   P. Riley

A SECOND BIOLOGY COURSE   P. T. Bunyan

MODELS FOR GCSE BIOLOGY   J. W. Garvin

SKILLS IN ADVANCED BIOLOGY
    VOLUME 1 DEALING WITH DATA
    J. W. Garvin

SKILLS IN ADVANCED BIOLOGY
    VOLUME 2 OBSERVING, RECORDING
    AND INTERPRETING
    J. W. Garvin, J. D. Boyd

Basic Biology Questions for Standard Grade

C. Rouan and B. J. Rouan

Stanley Thornes (Publishers) Ltd

© C. Rouan and B. J. Rouan 1990.

All rights reserved. No part of this publication may be reproduced or transmitted in any form or by any means, electronic or mechanical, including photocopy, recording, or any information storage and retrieval system, without permission in writing from the publisher or under licence from the Copyright Licensing Agency Limited. Further details of such licences (for reprographic reproduction) may be obtained from the Copyright Licensing Agency Limited, of 33-4 Alfred Place, London WC1E 7DP.

First published in 1990 by
Stanley Thornes (Publishers) Ltd
Old Station Drive
Leckhampton
CHELTENHAM GL53 0DN
England

British Library Cataloguing in Publication Data

Rouan, C.
  Basic biology questions for standard grade
  1. Biology,—Questions & answers—For schools
  I. Title   II. Rouan, B. J.
  574'.076

ISBN 0-7487-0452-3

Typeset by Blackpool Typesetting Services Limited.
Printed and bound in Great Britain at The Bath Press, Avon.

Contents

Topic 1: The biosphere — 1

1. Investigating an ecosystem — 2
2. How an ecosystem works — 12
3. Control and management — 23

Topic 2: The world of plants — 31

1. Introducing plants — 32
2. Growing plants — 36
3. Making food — 48

Topic 3: Animal survival — 57

1. The need for food — 58
2. Reproduction — 68
3. Water and waste — 75
4. Responding to the environment — 79

Topic 4: Investigating cells — 83

1. The structure of cells — 84
2. Diffusion and Osmosis — 87
3. Cell division — 92
4. Enzymes — 94
5. Respiration — 97

Topic 5: The body in action — 103

1. Movement — 104
2. The need for energy — 106
3. Co-ordination — 119
4. Changing levels of performance — 127

Topic 6: Inheritance — 131

1. Variation — 132
2. What is inheritance? — 133
3. Genetics and society — 141

Topic 7: Biotechnology 145
1. Living factories 146
2. Problems and profit of waste 148
3. Reprogramming microbes 157

Preface

Biological science, by the very nature of the subject, has an intrinsic appeal to children of all ages and abilities. However, interest can wane when faced with some of the more difficult demands of public examinations. Success and motivation go hand in hand.

The pressures on a teacher's time are considerable and increasing. There is a constant demand for exercises that are effective, stimulating and also relatively easy to correct and evaluate.

The questions in this book have been written specifically to meet the demands of the Scottish Certificate of Education Standard Grade Biology syllabus, at both general and credit levels.

For many pupils a minimum body of knowledge is essential before they are able to tackle with confidence the more demanding questions involving, for example, the analysis of data. In designing a wide range of question styles and tasks we hope to help in the acquisition of a basic knowledge and understanding of the subject matter and also to further the development of such scientific skills as observation, measurement, interpretation and application.

The aims of this question book are as follows:

1. To provide a framework within which pupils can compile a useful set of correct notes by working through and completing the various assignments, either on their own or with the help of the teacher.
2. To develop a pupil-centred approach to learning.
3. To provide an opportunity to develop pupil skills in numeracy and literacy.
4. To provide stimulating and varied material which can reinforce and consolidate the basic biological facts needed for 16+ examinations, whether in tests or in homework or classwork assignments. It can also, of course, be used as a revision programme.
5. To provide material that can be useful to students independently preparing for a SCE Standard Grade in Biology.
6. To provide graded material that can be used in a mixed-ability or streamed class, so that all pupils, it is to be hoped, will achieve some degree of success.
7. To provide material that is easy to use, easy to mark, and can be used in a wide variety of different ways by the teacher.

Anticipating the difficulty some pupils may have with diagrams, we have simplified many of those essential to the syllabus. Although there are questions asking pupils to copy diagrams we expect that in many cases they will be traced.

C. Rouan
B. J. Rouan
Cheltenham 1990

Acknowledgements

The authors and publishers are grateful to:
Dr M. B. V. Roberts for permission to use the information on p. 149 and to base the following diagrams upon those used in *Biology for Life* (Thomas Nelson and Sons Ltd): pp. 73, 77 and 109.

We are also grateful to John Murray (Publishers) Ltd for permission to use an abridged passage from *A Pattern of Islands* by Arthur Grimble, to BBC Books for permission to use an adaptation of a passage from *The Ascent of Man* by J. Bronowksi on p. 142, and to the Scottish Examination Board for the specimen question on p. 80.

Many people have helped in the production of this book and we would like to thank all those who have read the manuscript at its various stages for their constructive criticisms. We would also like to thank Donna Evans for her early and stimulating involvement.

The idea of writing such a book was prompted by Michael Roberts and it is to him that we are particularly grateful, not only for his initial stimulus, but also for his constant support and encouragement. His comments on the manuscript have been invaluable.

Finally it is with pleasure that we thank our publishers Stanley Thornes: for their enthusiasm, patience and good humour, and indeed we thank all those involved in the design and production of the book.

Topic 1

The Biosphere

Topic 1 The biosphere

1 Investigating an Ecosystem

1. Copy and complete this sentence:

   The study of living things is called _____.

2. a) A **habitat** is a particular place where organisms live. Which of the places in the list below would you call a habitat?

aeroplane	cloud	field	hedgerow	litter-bin	pond
pebble	stream	statue	seashore	pavement	sun
motor car	rain	woodland	wind		

   b) Every habitat has certain conditions that make it suitable for some organisms to live in, but not others. Look at the following list of organisms and decide which of them would be found

   i)   in a woodland

   ii) on the seashore

   iii) in a pond

stickleback	oak-tree	woodpecker	crab	ladybird
oyster-catcher	heron	water-lily	leaf-hopper	winkle
badger	seaweed	water-boatman	limpet	bluebell

   c) The conditions in the habitat make up the **environment**.

   i) Decide which of the features in the list below are part of the **physical** (abiotic) environment and which are part of the **biological** (biotic) environment. Record your answer in a table with these headings:

Physical (abiotic) environment	Biological (biotic) environment

   predators   temperature   light intensity   food supply   humidity
   depth of water   saltiness of water   rainfall

   ii) Which of the above conditions are most important to a plant living in a wood?

   d) The organisms which live in a particular habitat are adapted to living there.

   i) Copy the sentence above.

   ii) Explain the meaning of the word 'adapted'.

   e) Look at the illustrations on the next page. Each one shows an organism in its natural habitat. Suggest *one* way in which each organism is adapted to living there.

Topic 1 The biosphere

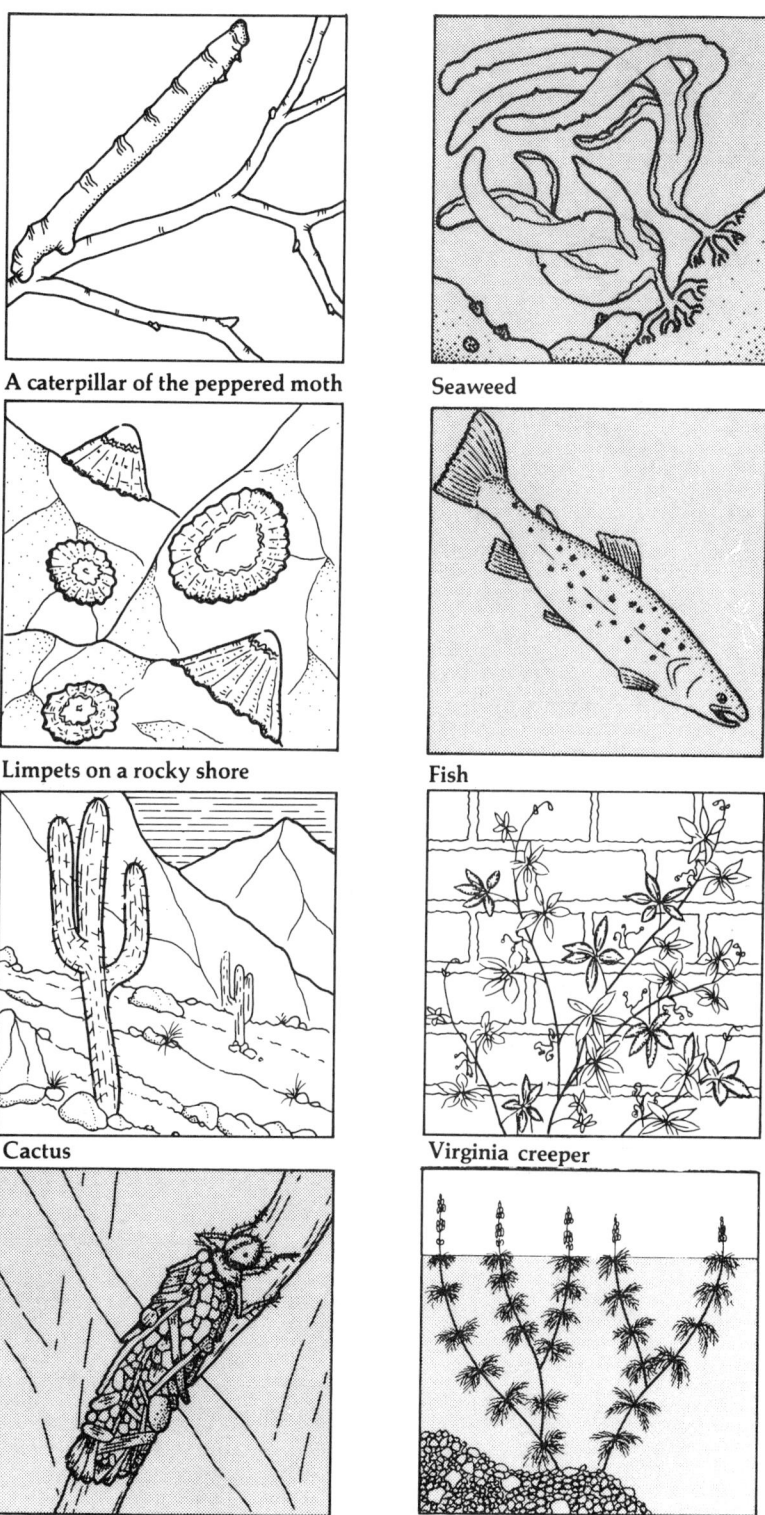

A caterpillar of the peppered moth

Seaweed

Limpets on a rocky shore

Fish

Cactus

Virginia creeper

A cased caddis-fly larva

Water milfoil

Topic 1 The biosphere

f) A **microhabitat** is a small part of a larger habitat, with a particular set of conditions. For example, a dead log in a wood is a microhabitat.

  i) Give another example of a microhabitat in a wood.

  ii) Give an example of a microhabitat in each of these habitats:

  stream   pond   rocky shore

3 The diagram below shows the layers in a wood.

a) Copy the diagram.

b) Which of the numbered regions corresponds to

  i) the field (herb) layer?

  ii) the canopy (tree) layer?

  iii) the shrub layer?

  iv) the ground layer?

c) Name one plant you would expect to find in *each* of the layers.

d) What effects will the canopy layer have on the conditions inside the wood in the summer?

4 The diagrams opposite show pieces of apparatus you might use to collect living things.

a) Briefly describe where and how you would use each one.

b) Describe *two* other methods of collecting organisms, one for water animals and one for land animals.

c) Make a list of at least *ten* other simple pieces of equipment that you might take with you when collecting living things.

Topic 1 The biosphere

Sweep net
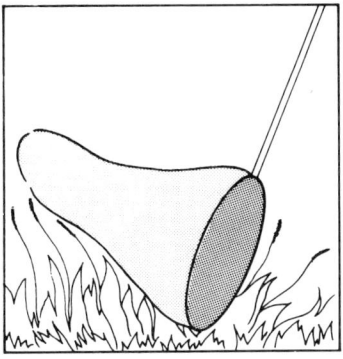

Pooter
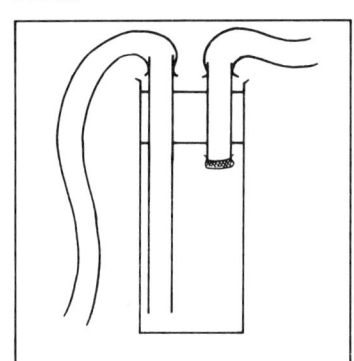

Pitfall trap

Plankton net
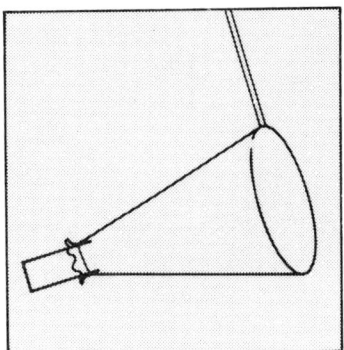

Beating-tray (or collecting-sheet)
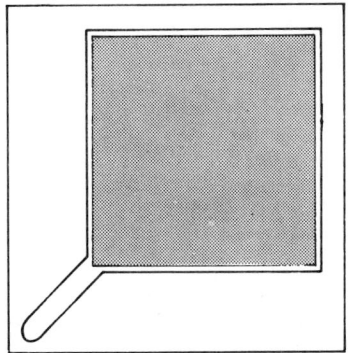

Mammal trap
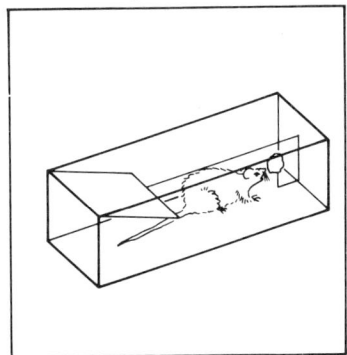

5 The diagram below shows a pitfall trap.

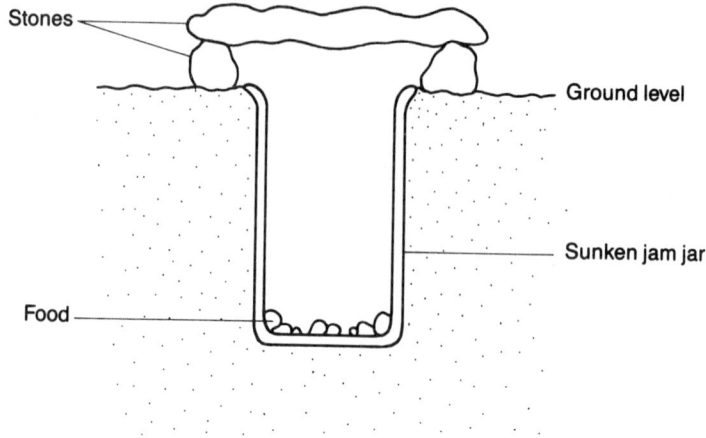

a) What types of animal would you expect to collect in this kind of trap?

b) Explain how you would use the trap to investigate

   i) whether a particular animal is more active on the forest floor at night than during the day

   ii) the sort of food beetles prefer

6 The apparatus shown below can be used to extract small animals from a sample of soil or leaf litter.

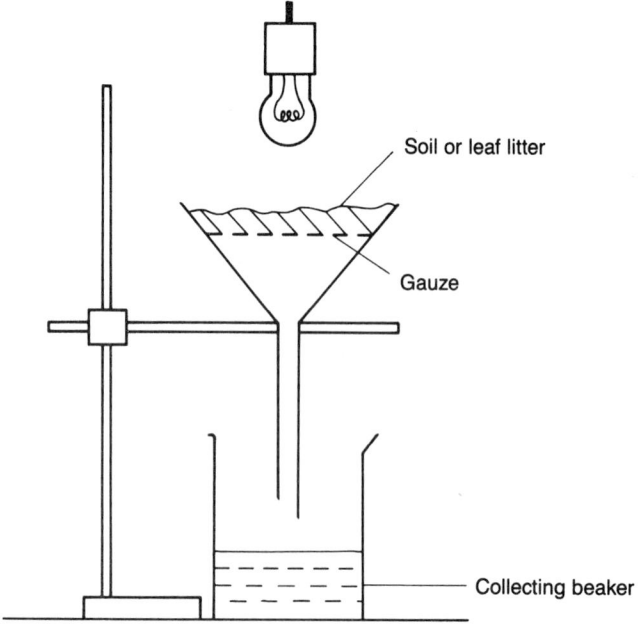

Topic 1 The biosphere

a) Draw and label the apparatus.

b) What *two* effects will the lamp have on the soil?

c) How do soil animals respond to the effect of the lamp?

d) Why should the lamp not be placed too close to the surface of the soil?

7 a) What is a 'quadrat'?

b) How would you use a quadrat to estimate the density of thistles in a field?

c) What are the main reasons for obtaining inaccurate results when using a quadrat?

d) The diagram below shows a grid made by dividing a quadrat frame into 100 squares. The grid has been used to sample a field and the shaded areas represent patches of grass. What is the percentage cover of the grass in this square metre of ground?

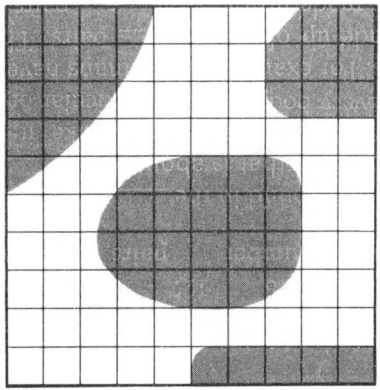

8 A student counted the number of thistles in twenty metre-square quadrats in a field. The results obtained are shown below.

Number of thistles	1	2	3	4	5	6
Number of quadrats with this number of thistles	2	4	7	5	3	1

a) Plot these results in a bar chart.

b) What is the average number of thistles per square metre?

c) What is the advantage of presenting these results as a bar chart?

9 Name a habitat you have studied. Describe exactly where this habitat was.

Topic 1   The biosphere

10 Draw a sketch map of the particular area you studied.

11 What physical conditions of the environment (abiotic factors) might control where organisms live in your habitat? Describe how you measured one of these factors.

12 a) Name *three* animals that you have found in your habitat.

   b) For each of the animals you have named give the following information:

   i)   How did you catch the animal?

   ii) Where in the habitat did you find it?

   iii) What features of the animal enabled you to identify it?

   iv) How is the animal adapted to living in this habitat?

13 a) Name one organism whose distribution was found to be uneven in your habitat. Describe its distribution.

   b) Describe how you investigated the distribution of this organism.

   c) What environmental condition or conditions may control the distribution of this organism?

14 During the year there will be changes in the organisms within your habitat. Write down *one* change that occurs in each of *three* named organisms. Present the information in a table as follows:

Organism	Change that occurs	Time of year
1.		
2.		
3.		

15 Suggest a problem faced by *one* named organism from your habitat and explain how it overcomes this problem.

Topic 1 The biosphere

16 This is an exercise in observation.

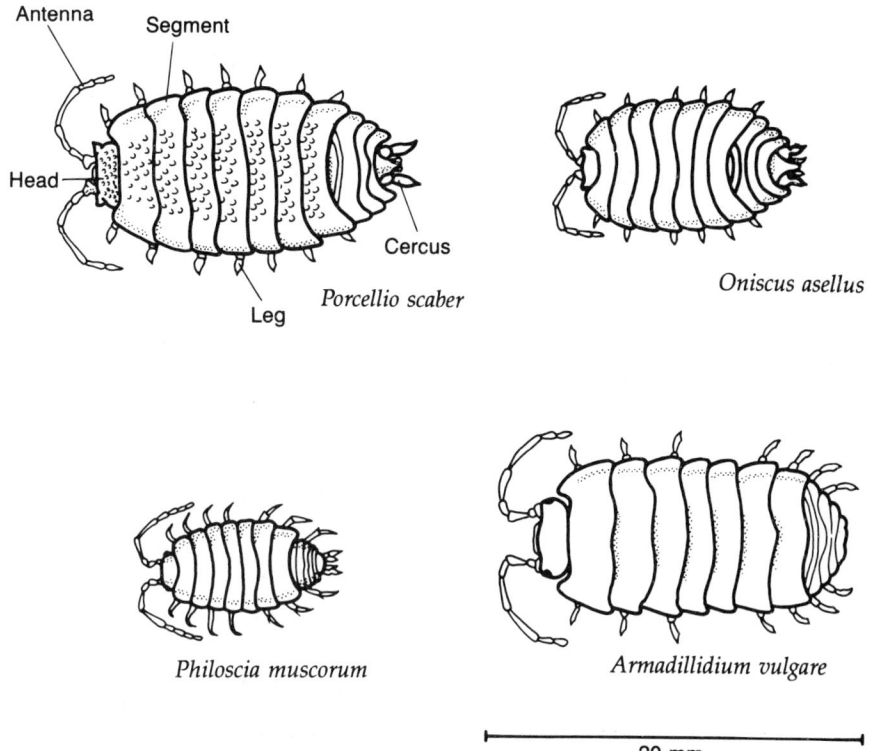

20 mm

a) Study the diagrams of the woodlice carefully, and then suggest *at least one* way in which each woodlouse differs from the other three. Ignore any differences in size.

Record your observations in a table with these headings.

Species	Observations

b) Why is size not a useful feature to choose when making such comparisons?

Topic 1 The biosphere

17 a) Look at the six illustrations of insects, labelled A–F. Use the key below to identify each of the insects.

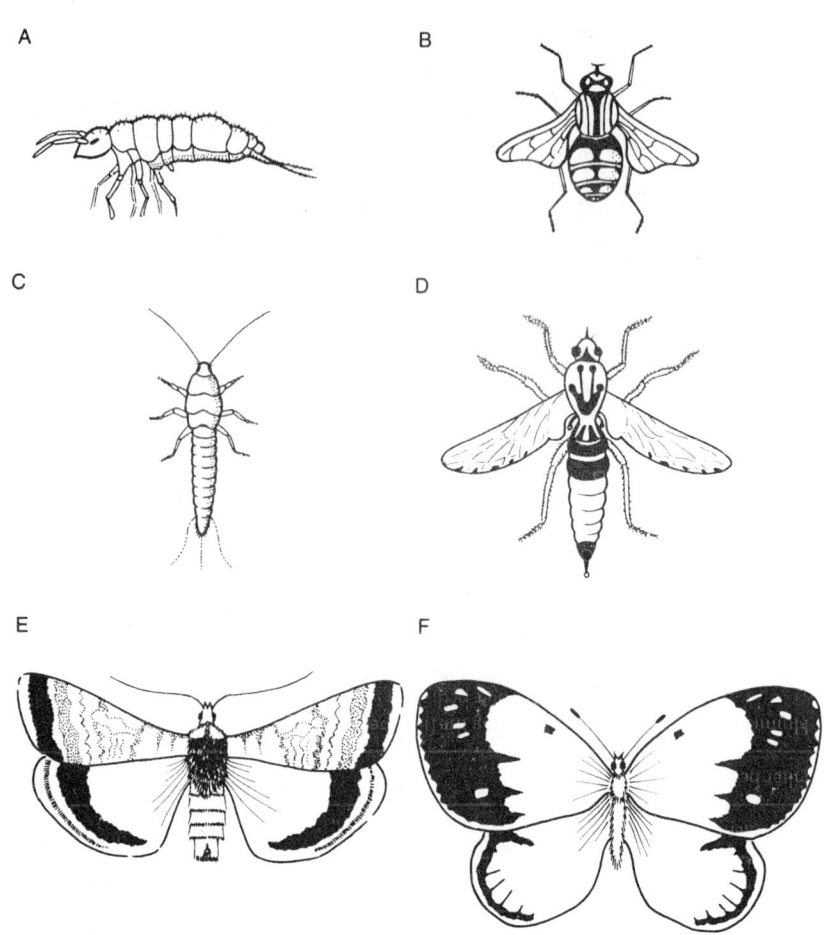

KEY

1. a) wings absent — go to number 2
   b) wings present — go to number 3
2. a) three tail filaments — silverfish
   b) two tail filaments — springtail
3. a) one pair of wings — go to number 4
   b) two pairs of wings — go to number 5
4. a) end of abdomen pointed — robber fly
   b) end of abdomen not pointed — go to number 6
5. a) club-shaped antennae — clouded yellow butterfly
   b) pointed antennae — large yellow moth
6. a) wings larger than body — green lacewing
   b) wings shorter than body — hoverfly

Topic 1 The biosphere

18 Study carefully the diagram below, which represents the zones of different plants growing on a sheltered rocky shore, and then answer the questions.

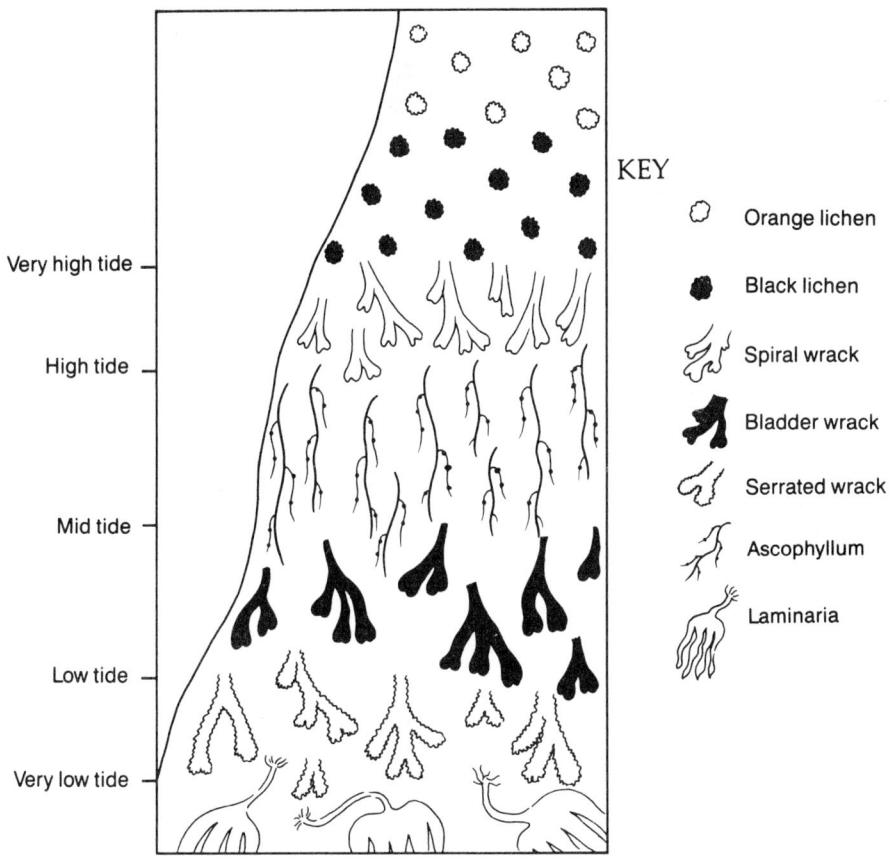

a) Which plants will not grow under sea-water?

b) Which plants are able to survive regular periods of exposure out of water?

c) Where would you find plants that are not very well adapted to being exposed to the atmosphere for long periods?

d) Which plants do not like to be exposed to the air at all?

19 The peppered moth lives in woods, feeding at night and resting on the lichen covered bark of trees during the daytime. The moth is usually speckled black and white, but some are so heavily speckled that they appear almost black. The moths are eaten by robins, thrushes and fly-catchers in the daytime.

Topic 1 The biosphere

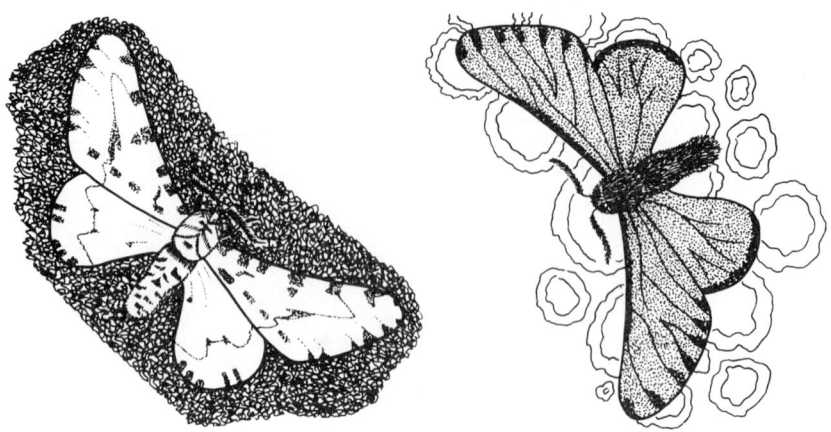

An investigation was carried out in which peppered moths were released in two different areas, and then some time later recaptured and counted. The results are shown in the table below. Study the results and then answer the questions.

	Dorset (agricultural area)		Birmingham (industrial area)	
	Speckled	Black	Speckled	Black
Number released	496	473	137	447
Number recaptured	62	30	18	123
Percentage recaptured	12.5	6.3	13.0	27.5

a) Which type of moth survived best in Dorset? Suggest a reason why.

b) Which type of moth survived best in Birmingham? Suggest a reason why.

c) What effect might the Clean Air Act have on future populations of the peppered moth in industrial areas?

2 How an Ecosystem Works

1 Each of the words in the following list is defined on the next page. Write out each of the definitions matched with the correct word from the list.

ecology   community   habitat   population   microhabitat
environment   ecosystem

Topic 1 The biosphere

a) The study of living things in relation to their environment.
b) A particular place where an organism lives.
c) The conditions, physical and biological, that are present in the place where an organism lives.
d) The living organisms of different species which live in a particular habitat.
e) A particular place within a habitat, with conditions to which certain organisms are adapted.
f) The number of individuals of a species that live in a particular habitat.
g) The interaction between the community and its non-living environment.

2 Copy and complete these sentences by choosing the correct words from inside the brackets:

a) A producer organism (makes food/eats other organisms/produces energy).
b) A consumer organism (makes food/eats other organisms/consumes light energy).
c) Producers are usually (animals/parasites/green plants).
d) A herbivore (eats plants/photosynthesises/eats other animals).
e) A carnivore (eats plants/photosynthesises/eats other animals).
f) The process by which the energy of sunlight is transferred to food is called (photosynthesis/respiration/symbiosis).
g) The process by which the energy is released from food is called (photosynthesis/respiration/symbiosis).
h) Microbes which feed on the dead bodies of animals and plants are called (parasites/decomposers/predators).

3 Consider this **food chain** and then answer the following questions:

plant → greenfly → frog → snake

a) Which organism is the producer?
b) Which organisms are the primary, secondary and tertiary consumers?
c) Which organism is a herbivore?
d) Which organisms are carnivores?
e) Which organism is the top carnivore?
f) What do the arrows in the food chain represent?

Topic 1 The biosphere

4 Each of the following lists of organisms shows the members of a food chain. In each list, arrange the organisms in their correct ecological order, starting with the producer.

  a) water-flea, stickleback, microscopic algae
  b) rose-bush, ladybird, greenfly
  c) fox, grass, rabbit
  d) snail, thrush, leaves

5 The following organisms can often be found living in the same habitat:

  caterpillar   earthworm   fox   greenfly   green plant   hawk
  ladybird   rabbit   small bird

  a) Construct a **food web** of the habitat. Use arrows to show the direction in which the energy is passing through the food web.
  b) Answer these questions about your food web:
   i) Which organism is the producer?
   ii) Name *two* organisms which are primary consumers.
   iii) Name *two* organisms which are secondary consumers.
   iv) Name an organism which is a herbivore.
   v) Name an organism which is a carnivore.
   vi) Which organism converts light energy into chemical energy?
   vii) What would be the possible consequences of a reduction in the number of rabbits?

6 After frequent visits to a pond near their school, and a long practical study, a class of pupils identified and observed many organisms. They gathered together the following information:

  Pond-snails feed on algae and pond-weed.
  Pond-skaters feed on water-fleas.
  Water-beetles feed on water-fleas and mayfly larvae.
  Roach feed on pond-snails, water-beetles and pond-skaters.
  Hydras feed on water-fleas.
  Mayfly larvae feed on algae.
  Water-fleas feed on algae.

  a) Construct a food web from this information.
  b) Name the producers in the food web.
  c) What happens to the animals and plants that die before being eaten by other animals?

Topic 1 The biosphere

7 List the organisms that you found in a habitat you have studied under three separate headings.

Producers	Herbivores	Carnivores

8 a) Draw *three* simple food chains from your habitat.

b) Draw a simple food web from your habitat.

9 This diagram represents the numbers of different organisms in a certain food chain:

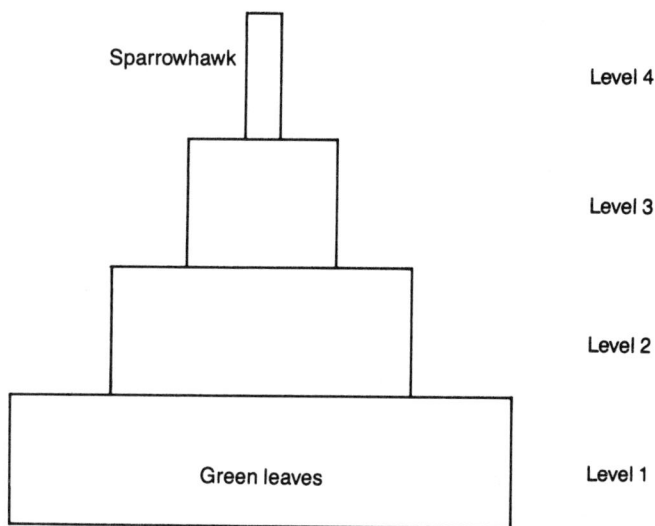

a) What is this type of diagram called?

b) Copy the diagram and suggest organisms which could be at levels 2 and 3.

c) Try to explain why there are fewer organisms at level 3 than at level 2.

10 Copy the following pyramids (A–D) of numbers and in each case choose the correct food chain which it represents. Write out the food chain below its pyramid.

16   Topic 1 The biosphere

C   D

Food chains:

Wheat → rat → flea   oak tree → aphid → bird

grass → rabbit → fox   cabbage → caterpillar → wasp parasite

11 a) What is 'biomass'?

b) What would a pyramid of biomass look like for examples B, C and D in question 10?

12 The diagram below shows what happens to the energy contained in the grass eaten by a young animal.

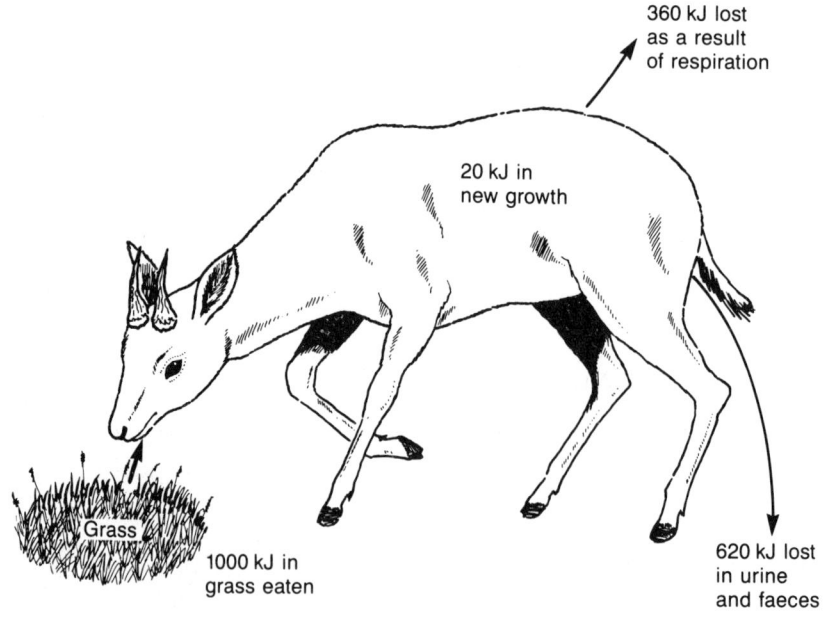

a) What percentage of the energy taken in by eating grass becomes part of the young animal?

b) What percentage of the energy taken in by eating grass is available to the next level in a food chain which includes this animal?

Topic 1 The biosphere

13 Here is a growth curve for a population of unicellular organisms. Copy it.

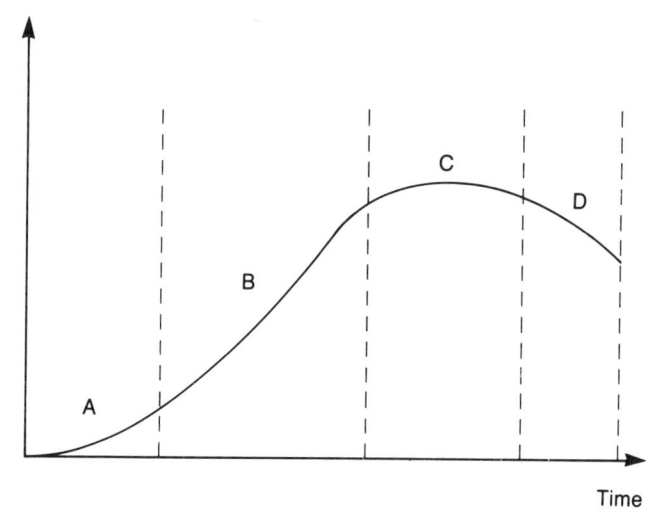

a) During which part of the curve, A, B, C or D, is the population growing most rapidly?

b) Complete these sentences by including the correct word or words from inside the brackets:

During stage A, growth of the population is very (slow/rapid).

During stage B, new cells are being produced far more (slowly/rapidly) than old cells are dying.

During stage C, new cells are being produced and old cells are dying (at the same time/at the same rate).

During stage D, old cells are dying more (rapidly/slowly) than new cells are being produced.

c) Suggest two changes in the environment of the cells which would cause the population growth to slow down.

14 The table below gives the world human population at various times since 1650.

Year AD	Approximate world population (millions)
1650	500
1850	1000
1900	1500
1925	2000
1950	2500
1960	3000
1975	4000
2000	?

a) Plot these data on graph paper, putting 'Year AD' on the horizontal axis beginning at 1600 and 'Number of people' on the vertical axis. Include the year 2000 on your time scale.

b) What would you predict to be the world human population in the year AD 2000?

c) How many years did it take the population to increase from
   i)   1000 million to 2000 million?
   ii) 2000 million to 3000 million?
   iii) 3000 million to 4000 million?

d) Make a list of the factors that normally stop animal populations from growing indefinitely.

e) For each of these factors, suggest a reason why it has failed to control the human population.

f) Write a short essay about the effects that the increasing human population has on the earth. Include comments on food, resources, pollution, wildlife, crime and living-space.

g) Why do you think the populations of developed countries, e.g. USA and Western Europe, are levelling off, whereas those of developing countries are continuing to rise at a very fast rate?

15 Read the following account of an experiment and then answer the questions:

Flies were sprayed with insecticide and some died. The survivors were counted and then allowed to breed. The next generation was sprayed with an insecticide. The survivors were again counted and then allowed to breed. The experiment was repeated for eight generations and the results recorded in the bar graph below.

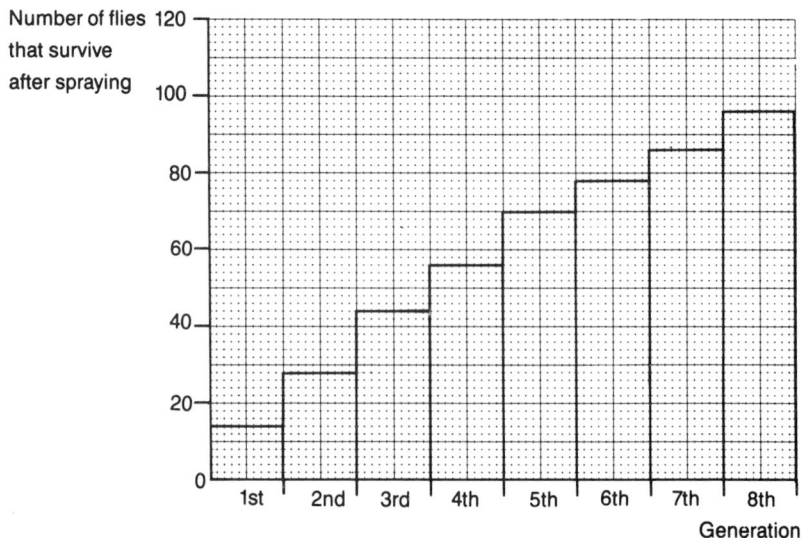

Topic 1 The biosphere

a) How many flies were alive during the third generation?
b) What do you notice about the number of flies that survive each spraying?
c) Give a reason for your answer to part b).
d) Give *two* reasons why the use of insecticides is not the best way of destroying pests.

16

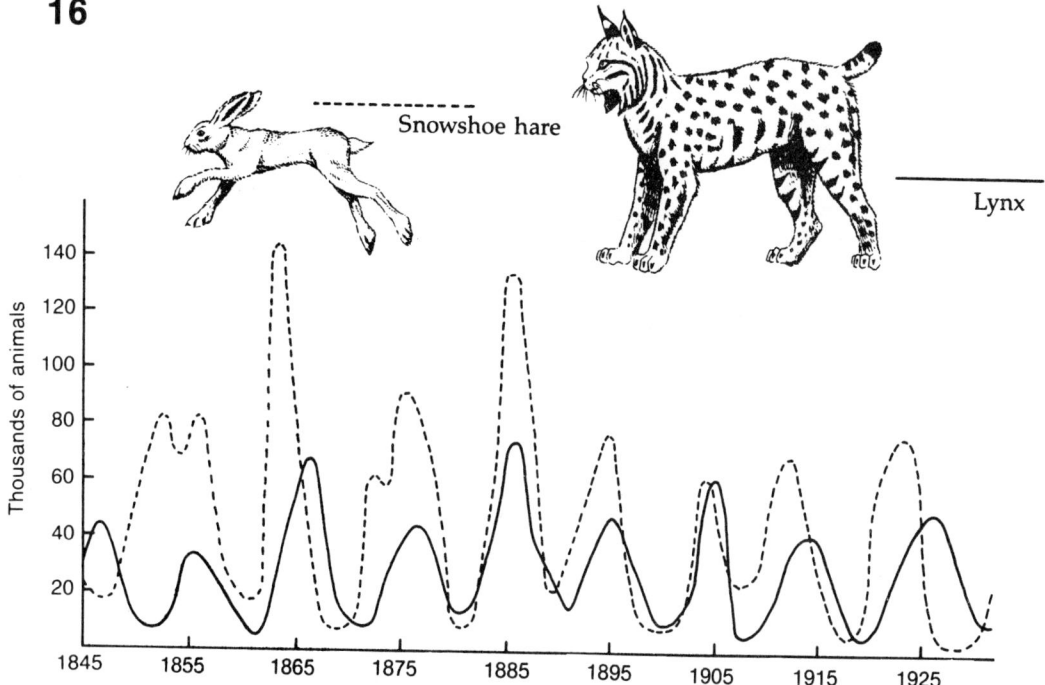

Variations in the populations of snowshoe hare and lynx in Northern Canada

The graph above shows changes in population numbers of snowshoe hares and lynx over eighty years in Northern Canada. Study the graph carefully and then answer the following questions (a–h).

a) How many hares were there in 1885?
b) How many lynx were there in 1885?
c) i) Suggest what hares eat.
   ii) Suggest what lynx eat.
d) What happened to the numbers of lynx as the hare population increased? Explain your observation.
e) What effect did large numbers of lynx have on the hare population? Explain your observation.
f) What happened to the numbers of lynx as the hare population fell?

g) How might this information on the changing populations of hares and lynx in Northern Canada have been collected?

h) What does this information tell you about the relationship between a predator and its prey?

17

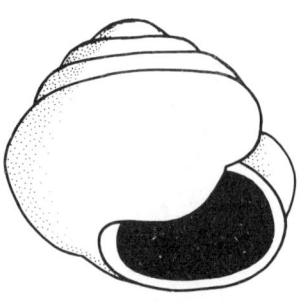
Unbanded

Banded

The above are drawings of a banded and an unbanded variety of the snail species *Cepaea nemoralis*. Random samples of these snails were collected from two different sites and the numbers recorded as shown in the following table.

Site	Number of snails	
	Banded	Unbanded
Grassland	29	70
Under hedgerows	89	10

a) How might random samples have been collected?

b) Suggest two hypotheses to account for the relative abundance of banded snails under hedgerows.

c) Design a simple experiment to test one of your hypotheses.

18 Read this passage and then answer the questions.

In the 1860s the orange orchards of California were threatened by an insect pest which had been accidentally introduced from Australia. All the insecticides known then were useless against the insects because these had a wax-like cuticle which was resistant to sprays. It was eventually found that in Australia the number of these insects was kept down by a small species of ladybird. The Australian ladybirds were released into the American orange orchards and within two years the insects had been brought under control and the orange orchards were saved.

Topic 1 The biosphere

a) Why did the insect become a pest in California?
b) Why was it not a pest in Australia?
c) Why could the insect not be controlled by insecticides in the 1860s?
d) How was the insect finally brought under control?
e) What is the advantage of using biological control?
f) What are the possible problems of using biological control?
g) Give *two* other examples of humans using biological control to keep down a pest.

19 There are living organisms in the soil which are too small to be seen with the naked eye or even a hand-lens.

a) Name *two* different groups of such organisms.
b) What do they feed on?
c) What benefit are these micro-organisms to larger plants growing in the soil?
d) Give a detailed account, with diagrams, of how you would set up an experiment to show that these micro-organisms are present in soil. Point out any controls you would need, and describe the results you would expect.

20 a) Construct a table to show the conditions required for decay to occur. Your table should look like this:

Conditions required	Reason
1. heat	So bact can grow
2. oxygen	
3. water	So bact can grow
4. oxygen	For aerobic bact and fungi

b) Explain why
   i) extinct mammoths have been found undecayed in Siberia. *Ice – too cold for bacteria*
   ii) the bodies of Egyptian kings have been found undecayed in the pyramids.
   iii) biologists keep specimens of animals and plants in alcohol. *bacteria cannot live in alcohol*

Topic 1 The biosphere

21 a) Copy these sentences about the **carbon cycle**. Choose words from the following list and fill in the gaps. (The words may be used more than once.)

plants   decay   respiration   animals   photosynthesis   combustion carbon dioxide

i) _plants_ use carbon dioxide and water to make sugars by the process of _photosynthesis_.

ii) _plants_ and _animals_ break down sugars into carbon dioxide and water by the process of _respiration_.

iii) When animals and plants die, their bodies _decay_.

iv) During the process of decay, microbes return _CO2_ to the atmosphere.

v) Carbon dioxide is removed from the air by the process of _photosyn_ and put back into it by the processes of _respiration_ and _combustion_.

vi) When fossil fuels are burnt, carbon dioxide is returned to the atmosphere. This process is called _combustion_.

b) Name *two* fossil fuels. How are they formed? _Coal, oil_ _Compressed trees_ _Plankton_

c) Draw a diagram to show how the processes of **photosynthesis, respiration, combustion** and **decay** are involved in the carbon cycle.

22

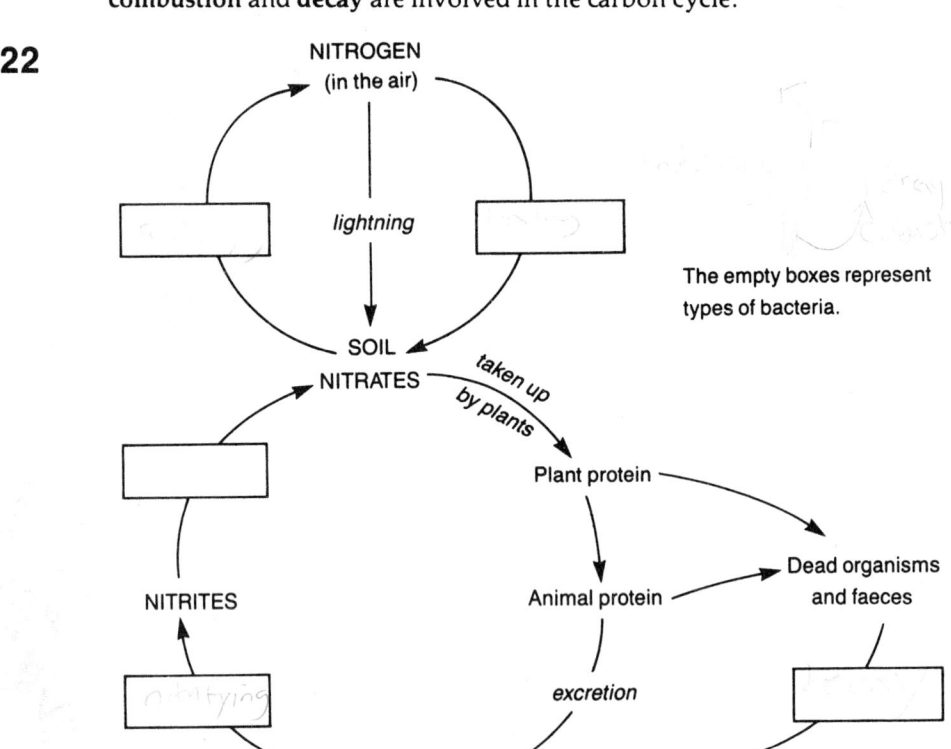

Topic 1 The biosphere

The bacteria involved in the **nitrogen cycle** are:

    decay bacteria   nitrifying bacteria   nitrogen-fixing bacteria
    denitrifying bacteria

a) Copy the diagram opposite, which summarises the nitrogen cycle, and in the boxes write the names of the bacteria active at each stage.

b) In the nitrogen cycle, which of the bacteria are helpful and which are unhelpful?

unhelpful – denitrifying
All others helpful

23 Answer these questions about the nitrogen cycle:

a) Why is nitrogen essential for life? *essential element in proteins & DNA*

b) How do

    i) plants ← *nitrates from soil (then also from animals)*

    ii) animals *from plants and other animals*

obtain nitrogen?

c) Why does the nitrogen cycle work better in well aerated soil? *bacteria grow better?*

d) Why is soil made more fertile by growing peas, beans or clover? *get nitrates put into soil by agrobacterium*

e) During a flood the soil will lose nitrates. Why? *washed away water soluble*

---

3 Control and Management

1 Look for an example of **pollution** in the area where you live.

  a) Say exactly where you found the pollution.

  b) What caused the pollution? Say what the pollutant was, and describe the source of it (where it came from).

  c) What are the effects of this pollution on

    i) the environment?

    ii) plants and animals (including humans)?

2 a) One cause of air pollution in Great Britain is smoke. What process produces the smoke?

  b) The three main pollutants in the smoke are carbon particles (soot), carbon dioxide gas and sulphur dioxide gas.

    i) Which of these causes blackening of buildings and trees?

    ii) Which of them dissolves to form acid rain?

iii) What effect does acid rain have on buildings?

iv) What effect does acid rain have on plants and animals?

v) How could smoke produced in Great Britain be the cause of acid rain damage in Scandinavia?

vi) What steps can be taken to reduce the production of acid rain?

c) What effect do the pollutants in smoke have on our health?

d) What is smog?

e) How has pollution from smoke been reduced in recent years?

3 Consider the motor vehicle:

Topic 1 The biosphere

a) What effect do motor vehicles have on our environment? Before you answer this question think about the following:

  **the roads required to carry traffic   traffic noise and vibration
  the effect on the countryside of beauty spots easily reached by road
  the effect on human health**

b) Over three million vehicles crowd into Los Angeles each day. What effect does this have on the atmosphere, and why?

c) How do motorway planners try to reduce the effects of these roads on the environment?

d) How can pollution by motor cars be reduced?

4 Cockshoot Broad is a lake in Norfolk. The map below shows that water flows into Cockshoot Broad from the River Bure. The area is surrounded by farmland that slopes down to the lake.

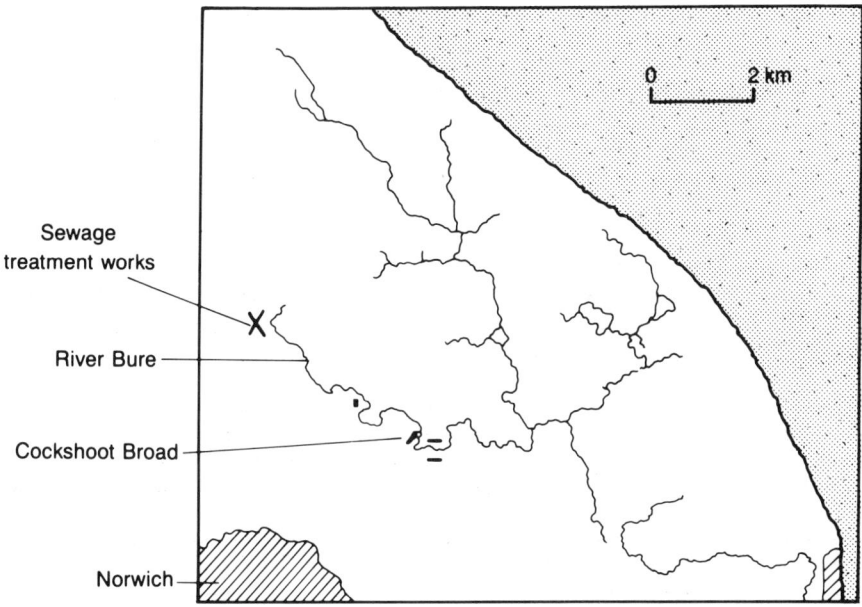

In recent years there has been a large increase in the levels of phosphate and nitrate in the waters of Cockshoot Broad.

a) Suggest where these chemicals could have come from.

b) When high levels of nitrate and phosphate pollute a lake or river, a series of changes takes place in the water, resulting in the death of many fish.
   Rewrite the following sentences in the correct order to give a summary of the changes which occur.

Nitrates and phosphates provide essential minerals for the growth of microscopic algae.

Populations of bacteria increase and use up large amounts of oxygen.

Nitrates and phosphates pollute the water.

Oxygen levels in the water drop sharply.

The water becomes green and cloudy as the numbers of algae rise.

Fish die due to lack of oxygen.

Many algae then die and provide food for decay bacteria.

c) Why is there a build-up of dead organic matter on the bottom of polluted lakes and rivers?

d) In some regions the level of nitrates in drinking water has increased. Why does this give cause for concern?

5 The diagram opposite shows freshwater animals associated with organic pollution. Study the diagram and answer the questions.

a) What happens to the concentration of oxygen in the water as sewage enters the river?

b) Which of the organisms shown can only survive in very polluted water?

c) Which organisms can only survive in very clean water?

d) What is a 'pollution-indicator organism'?

6 Copy and complete this table, which shows some of the harmful consequences of human activities and past mistakes, and possible remedies. (The first one has been done for you as an example.)

Human activities	Consequences	Remedies
Burning fossil fuels	respiratory diseases and blackening of buildings	smokeless zones, alternative fuels
	decrease in number of whales	
	destruction of tropical rain forests	
	pollution of river water	
	mutations in sex cells of ovary and testis	
	damage to inner ear	
	photochemical smog	
	reduction in variety of British wildlife	

Topic 1 The biosphere

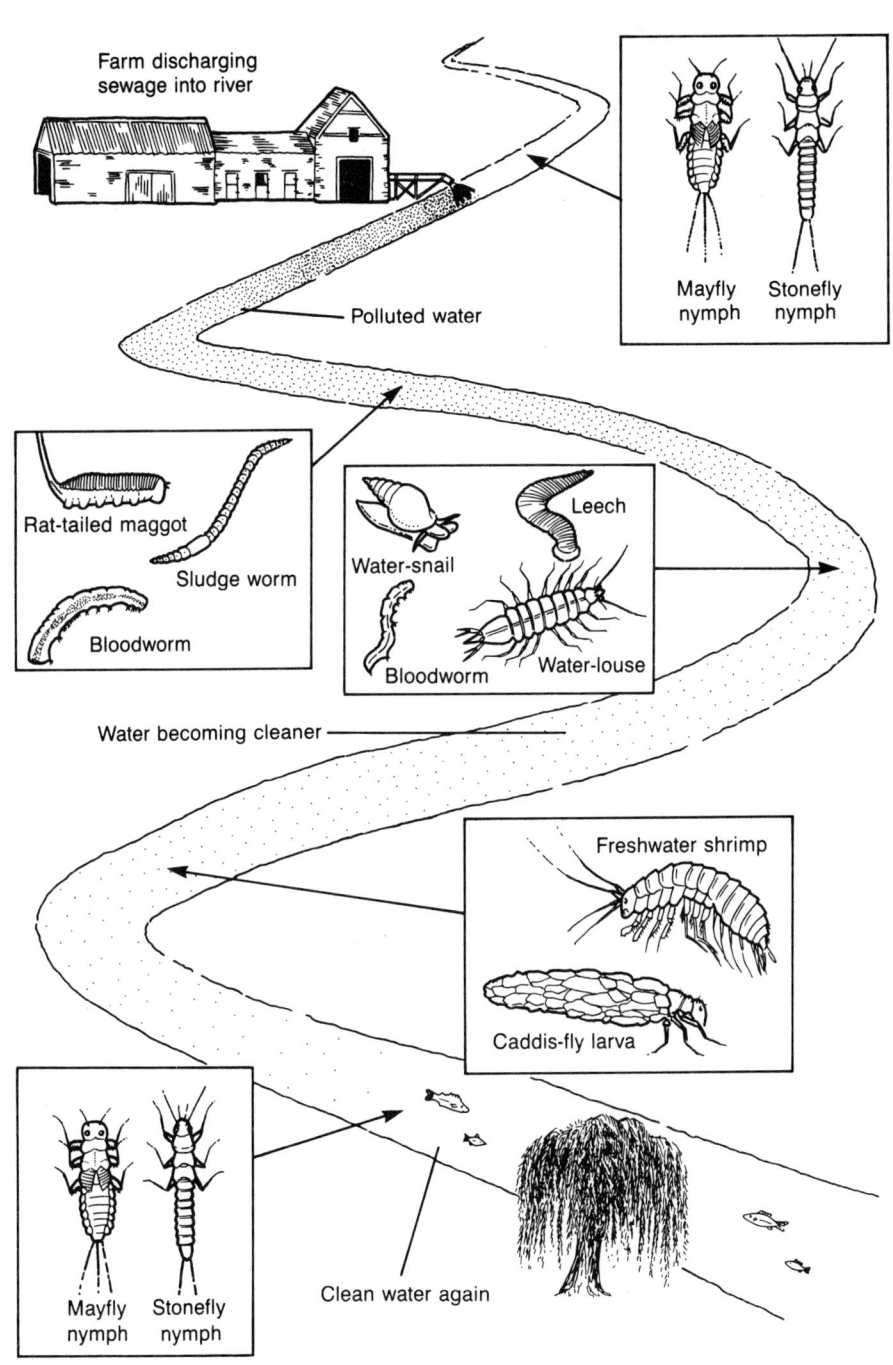

7 Read the following passage and then answer the questions that follow:

> An area of poor agricultural land which had always been used for rough grazing of sheep during summer was to be 'improved' by ploughing and sowing with good grazing grasses. Conservationists opposed the change on two grounds: firstly that the area was of special scientific interest because of the rare heathland plants and animals; secondly because they said that the mixture of flowers indicated a soil of low mineral content, making it of little use for farming.
>
> A group of scientists surveyed the area. Firstly they sampled the vegetation using quadrats, and then made a line transect from the poor agricultural grazing through to previously 'improved' grassland. The invertebrates and vertebrates were sampled throughout the area. Lastly numerous soil samples were taken and tested.
>
> The final report sent in by the scientists indicated that the variety of flowers was good and that the variety of animals was also good, the level of soil minerals was low, but that the 'improved' grassland yielded good grazing, superior in quality to the rough grazing.

a) Why did the farmer want to improve the grassland?

b) i) Suggest two reasons why ploughing might 'improve' the grassland.

ii) Suggest two other ways in which the farmer might 'improve' his grassland.

c) Why did the conservationists oppose the change?

d) i) What is a quadrat?

ii) Explain how quadrats could be used to survey the vegetation.

e) i) Explain how the scientists would have made the line transect.

ii) What do you think the line transect was used to show?

f) i) Suggest two ways in which the invertebrates might be sampled.

ii) Suggest two ways in which the vertebrates might be sampled.

8 Read this passage about modern farming methods and then answer the questions:

> Any expensive piece of farm machinery is only a profitable investment if it is constantly in use. Farms have become larger and hedges have been ripped up. Many farmers do not keep cattle and so have no farmyard manure. Large amounts of chemical fertilisers have to be used. This has the effect of making some soils thin and dusty, particularly when cereals are grown year after year. When the weather is wet, such soils become infertile and waterlogged. In dry and windy conditions the soil blows away in dust storms.

Topic 1 The biosphere

a) What is meant by 'a profitable investment'?
b) Name an 'expensive piece of farm machinery'.
c) Why do you think that many farmers do not keep cattle?
d) Suggest *two* advantages and *two* disadvantages of using
   i) farmyard manure
   ii) chemical fertilisers
e) How can cereal farmers reduce the effects of artificial fertilisers on the soil?
f) Why is it necessary to grow crops such as wheat in very large quantities?

9 The following table compares the total hedge length dug up by farmers during the period 1945–72, in five English counties. Study the table and then answer the questions.

County	Percentage of hedge removed	Main agricultural activity
Huntingdonshire	38	crops
Dorset	10	dairy
Herefordshire	10	mixed
Yorkshire	15	crops
Warwickshire	7	dairy, mixed

a) Suggest reasons why more hedges have been removed in Huntingdonshire and Yorkshire.
b) Suggest *two* reasons why hedges might be useful to farmers.
c) Why are hedges useful to wild animals?
d) Why does growing crops in small fields reduce the effect of pests?
e) Why is it better to space out the plants in a field?
f) Many farmers now leave a corner of a field uncultivated. What do they hope to gain by doing this?
g) Suggest *three* ways in which modern farming has harmed wildlife.
h) Explain how the removal of one animal from a food chain or web can upset the balance of nature in a community.

10 a) What do we mean by 'conservation' when referring to our environment?
b) Try to find out the names of at least two organisations concerned with conservation in Britain.
c) What is a nature reserve?

d) Try also to find the names of

   i) two plants

   ii) two birds

   iii) two other vertebrates

   that are protected by law in Britain. Why are they protected?

e) Why is it important not to pick wild flowers in the countryside?

Topic 2

The world of plants

1 Introducing Plants

1 The table below lists differences between animals and plants. Copy and complete it by giving a reason for each difference.

Typical animal (e.g. a frog)	Typical plant (e.g. a buttercup)	What is the reason for this difference?
Has feeding structures such as mouth and gut	Lacks feeding structures	
Lacks chlorophyll	Has chlorophyll	
Not rooted in the ground	Is rooted in the ground	
Moves around	Does not move around	
Has nerves and muscles	Lacks nerves and muscles	
Has sense receptors such as eyes and ears	Lacks sense receptors	

2 The drawings opposite illustrate a variety of plants. Study them and answer the questions.

a) Which of the plants are **aquatic** (live in water)?

b) Which one is not an example of a true plant as it has no chlorophyll?

c) Which of the plants produce seeds?

d) Which of the **terrestrial** (and-dwelling) plants has no true roots, stems or leaves?

e) Which of the plants is a **conifer**?

f) Which of the plants are **flowering plants**?

g) Which of the flowing plants are

i) **monocotyledons**?

ii) **dicotyledons**?

Topic 2 The world of plants

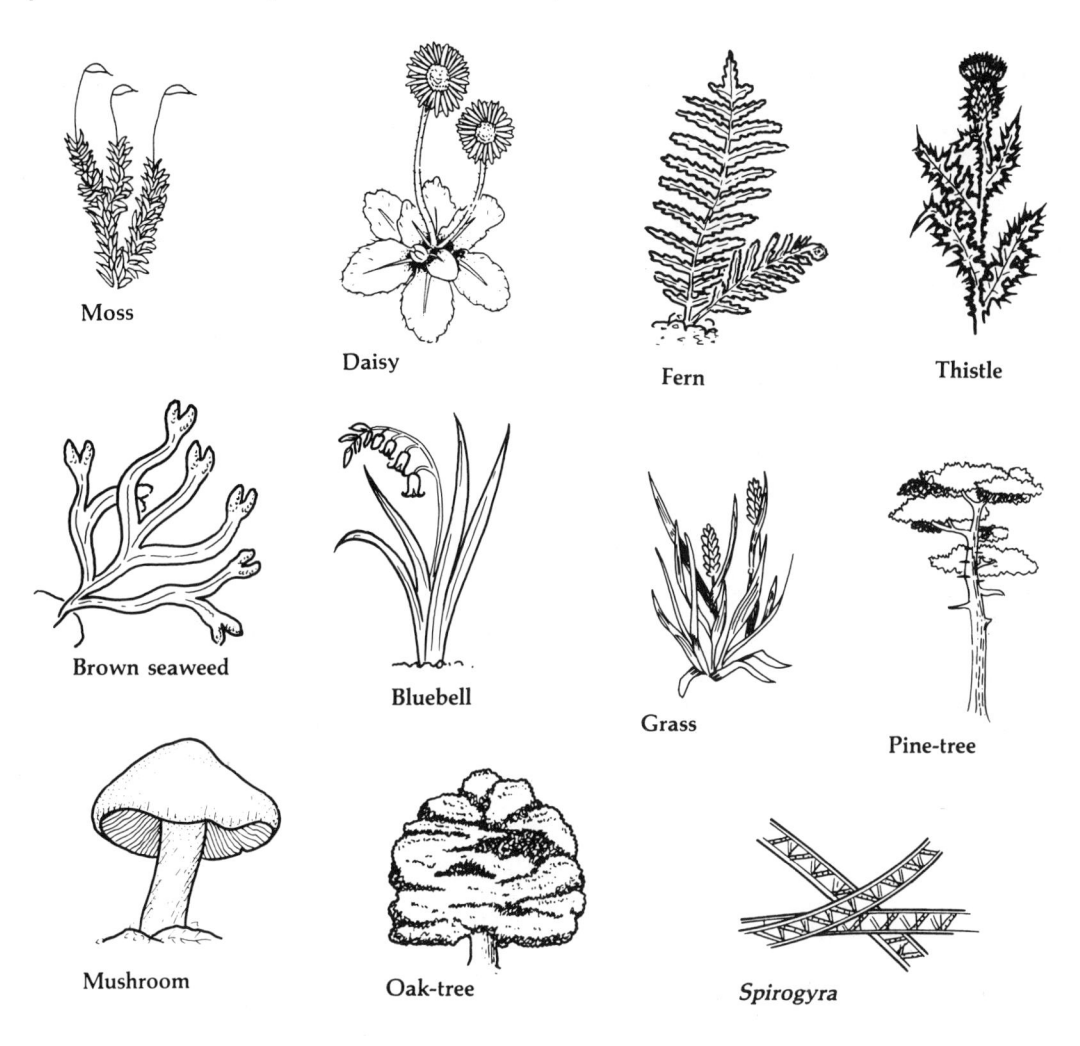

Moss

Daisy

Fern

Thistle

Brown seaweed

Bluebell

Grass

Pine-tree

Mushroom

Oak-tree

Spirogyra

3 Complete these sentences, which describe the structure of a flowering plant such as the one in the diagram on the next page.

a) The plant is made up of two main parts, the _____ and the _____.

b) The _____ is above the ground and the _____ is below the ground.

c) The main root is called the _____.

d) Near the tip of each side root is a covering of _____ _____.

e) At the tip of the shoot there is an _____ bud where growth takes place.

f) _____ are flat and green.

g) Each leaf is attached to the stem by a short _____ _____.

h) Nodes are the points where _____ are attached to the stem.

i) The small bud at a node is called an _____ bud.

Topic 2   The world of plants

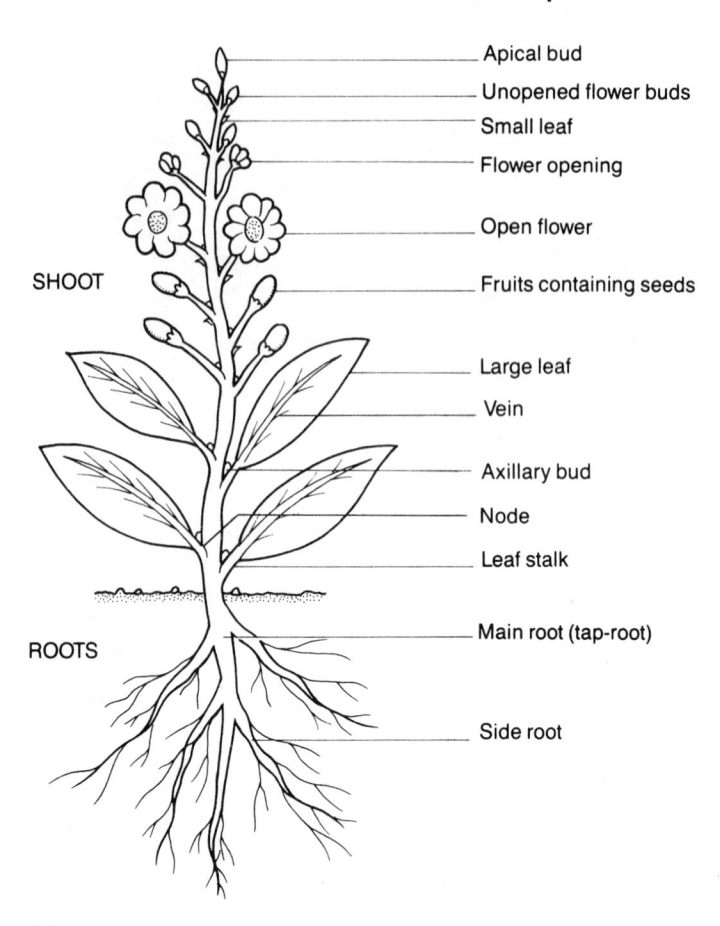

Apical bud
Unopened flower buds
Small leaf
Flower opening
Open flower
Fruits containing seeds
Large leaf
Vein
Axillary bud
Node
Leaf stalk
Main root (tap-root)
Side root

SHOOT
ROOTS

4 What jobs are carried out by
   a) the stem?
   b) the roots?
   c) the leaves?
   d) the flowers?
   e) the fruits?

5 Complete the following sentences by using either **'monocotyledons'** or **'dicotyledons'**, or both:
   a) The two main groups of flowering plants are _____ and _____.
   b) _____ have one seed leaf.
   c) _____ have two seed leaves.
   d) _____ have broad leaves with a network of veins.

Topic 2 The world of plants

e) _____ have narrow leaves with parallel veins.

f) _____ have a bundle of thin fibrous roots.

g) _____ have a main tap-root and short side roots.

6 a) Which of the plants shown in the diagram below is a monocotyledonous plant and which is a dicotyledonous plant?

b) What features of the plants shown in the diagram support your answer?

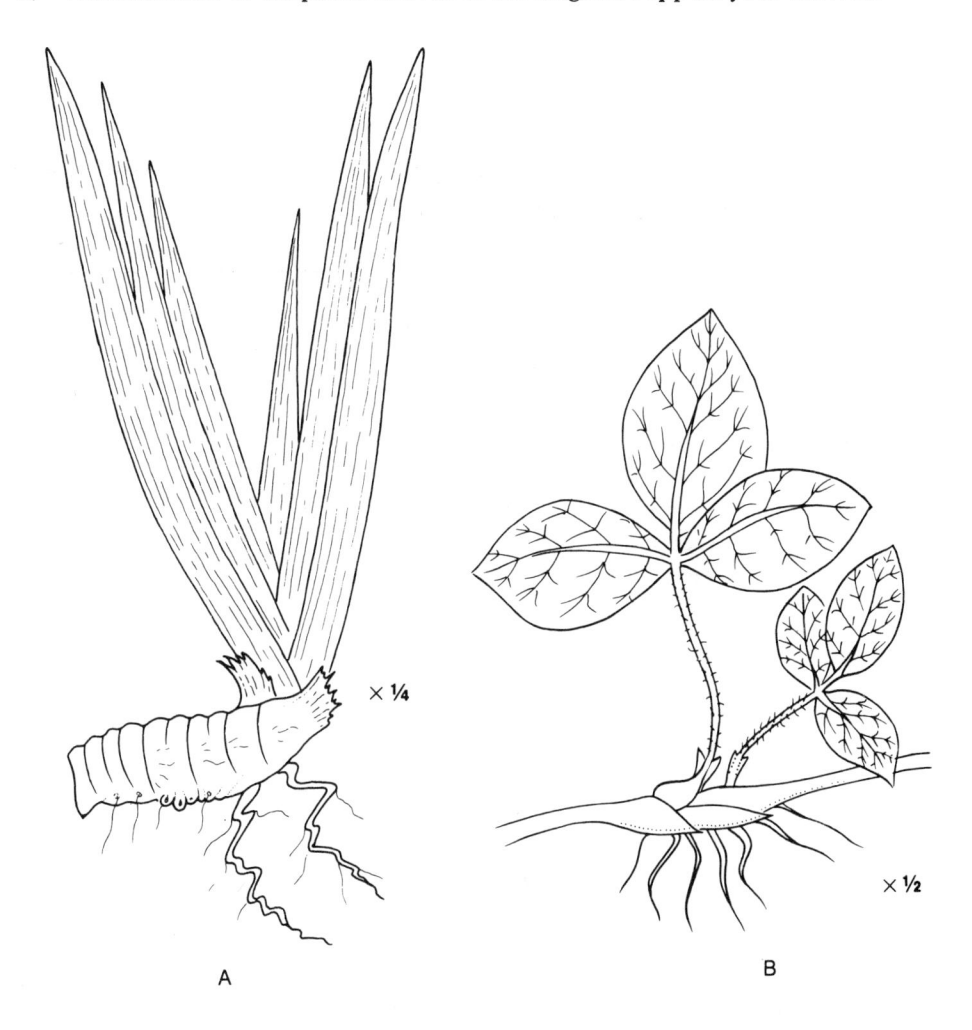

× ¼

× ½

A

B

7 Many useful products are obtained from plants. Answer the following questions (a–i) about useful plants and their products.

a) Name *two* plants grown for their vegetable oil. From which part of the plant does the oil come?

b) Which plants are grown to make sugar?

c) Perfumes are made using oils from plants. Give *one* example of a plant used to make perfume.

d) Name *two* drugs obtained from plants.

e) Why do we depend on plants for the meat in our diets as well as for the vegetables?

f) Give some examples of herbs and spices obtained from plants.

g) How is paper made?

h) Why should people be encouraged to use recycled paper?

i) Make a list of *ten* plants whose products are useful for some purpose other than food.

2 Growing Plants

1 This question is about the structure of seeds.

a) Match the word or words in the left-hand column with the descriptions in the right-hand column.

seed coat (testa)	the young shoot
embryo	protects the seed
plumule	stores food
radicle	consists of plumule and radicle
seed leaf (cotyledon)	the young root

b) Copy this diagram of half a broad bean seed. Replace the letters A to E with labels from this list:

plumule   radicle   embryo plant   seed coat   seed leaf

Half of a dormant broad bean seed

Topic 2 The world of plants

c) If you took a dry broad bean seed and soaked it, what differences would you expect there to be between the dry and the soaked seed? How can you explain them?

d) Complete this passage by choosing the correct words from inside the brackets:

If iodine solution is placed on the seed leaves of a broad bean, they will turn (yellow/black) because they contain (sugar/starch) which will feed the (embryo/seed) when it starts to grow.

2 Complete these sentences about seeds by choosing the correct word from inside the brackets:

a) Fruits and seeds are formed from the (flowers/leaves).

b) When seeds are dried out they are said to be (dormant/dead).

c) When they are (dead/dormant) seeds can survive summer drought and winter cold.

d) Broad bean seeds are found inside fruits called (shells/pods).

3 a) The germinating seeds shown in the apparatus below have been provided with **water, warmth** and **oxygen**. Using similar apparatus design an experiment to test the hypothesis that all three of these conditions are required for germination.

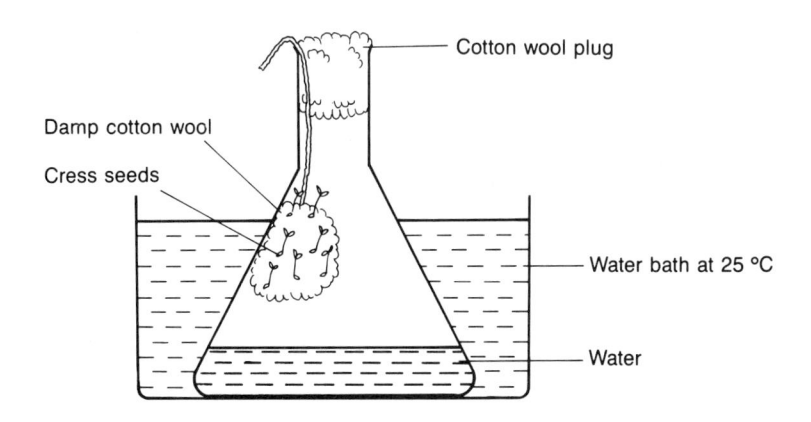

NB An alkaline solution of pyrogallol absorbs oxygen.

b) How might your experiment be modified to investigate the effect of a range of temperatures on the germination of cress seeds?

4 These questions are about the **germination** of the broad bean seed.

a) Copy this passage about the germination of a broad bean seed but include only the correct word from inside the brackets.

Before germination the broad bean seed must take in (food/water) mainly through a tiny hole called the (testa/micropyle). This causes the seed to (swell/shrivel) and the seed coat bursts open. The (embryo/seed leaf) starts to grow. The young (root/shoot) appears first and grows (downwards/upwards). The young (root/shoot) appears next and grows (upwards/downwards). Eventually the (root/shoot) breaks through the surface of the soil. The first green (leaves/flowers) appear. The young plant is called a (seedling/embryo).

b) i) Copy this diagram of a bean seedling:

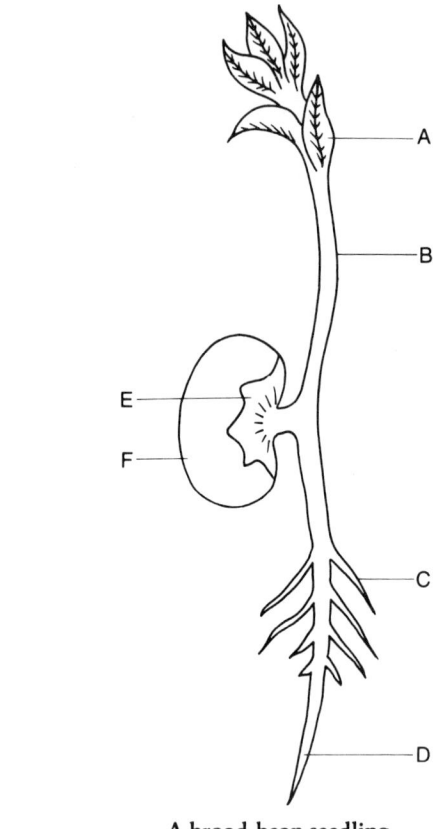

A broad bean seedling

Replace the letters A to F with labels from this list:

first green leaves   main root   side root   seed coat
seed leaf   stem

ii) Mark the position of the surface of the soil on your diagram.

Topic 2 The world of plants

5 Some information on the growth of a sunflower stem is given in the table below.

Age /days	7	14	21	28	35	42	49	56	63	70	77	84
Height /cm	16	34	62	98	135	172	206	228	247	251	254	255

a) Draw a graph of these results. Label the axes as shown.

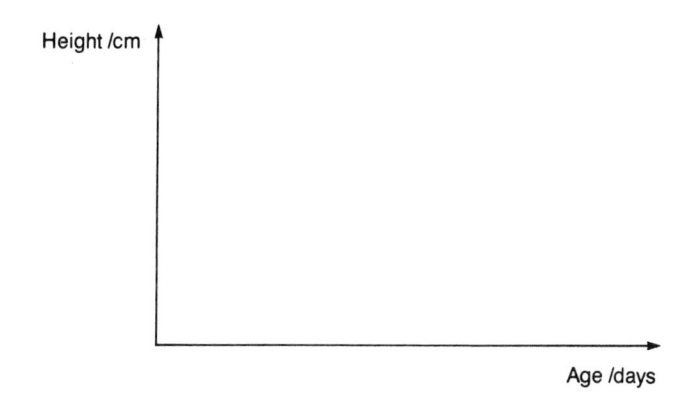

This is a **growth curve**.

b) Describe the shape of the growth curve.

c) What is the length of the stem after
   i)   10 days?
   ii) 30 days?
   iii) 46 days?
   iv) 80 days?

d) When is the stem growing
   i) most rapidly?
   ii) most slowly?

6 Pea seeds were planted in soil in seed boxes and given suitable conditions for germination. Twenty seedlings were removed each week, washed to remove any soil and then heated in an oven to 110 °C, until all the water had been removed. The batches of dry seedlings were then weighed to determine their mass. The results are shown on the next page.

Age /weeks	1	2	3	4	5	6	7
Dry mass of twenty seedlings /g	6	4	2	1	8	25	45

a) Plot a graph of these results. Label your axes as shown.

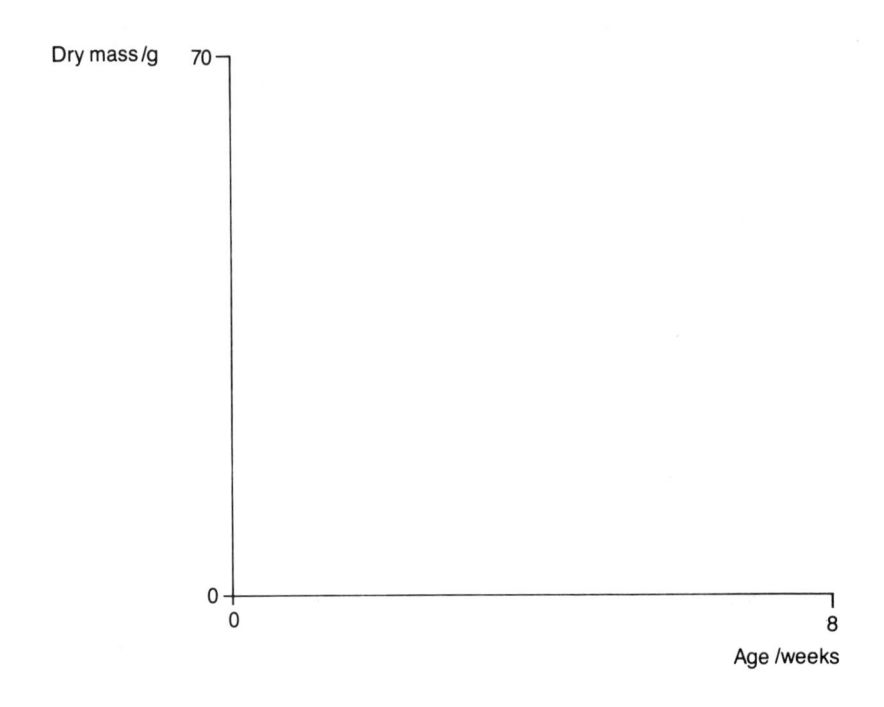

b) What is meant by 'dry mass'?

c) i) What happened to the dry mass of the seedlings during the first four weeks?

   ii) Why did the dry mass change during this time?

d) Use the graph to estimate the dry mass of twenty seedlings after eight weeks.

e) There is a rapid gain in dry mass during the final three weeks.

   i) What process makes this rapid gain possible?

   ii) Name *two* important substances used in this process.

f) i) How would you expect the results to differ if the experiment were carried out in the dark?

   ii) How many seeds would then have to be sown in order to get the results of this experiment?

Topic 2 The world of plants

7 a) Copy this diagram of a wallflower in section. Replace the letters A to H with labels from the following list:

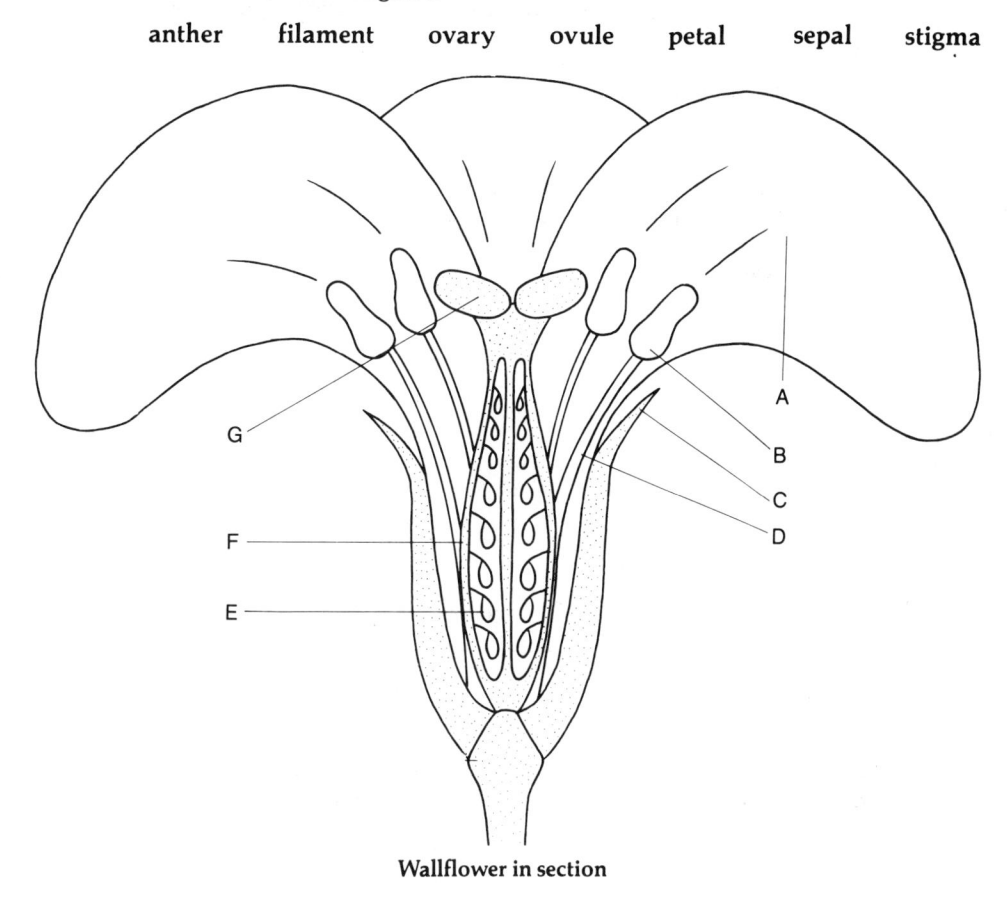

    anther   filament   ovary   ovule   petal   sepal   stigma

Wallflower in section

b) The wallflower is pollinated by insects. Which parts of the flower have the function of attracting insects?

8 Match the parts of a flower in the left-hand column with their correct functions in the right-hand column.

Parts of a Flower	Function
style	to support the anther
stigma	to produce pollen
pollen	to make a sugary liquid
petal	to receive pollen
nectary	to contain the male gamete
sepal	to attract insects
anther	to hold up the stigma
ovary	to protect the flower in bud
filament	to contain the female gametes

9 Copy and complete these two sentences:

a) The transfer of pollen from the anther to the stigma is called _____ .

b) The joining of the male nucleus from the pollen grain with the egg cell in the ovule is called _____ .

10 a) Copy this diagram of a carpel (the female part of a flower). Replace the letters A to F with labels chosen from this list:

egg cell   micropyle   ovary   ovule   stigma   style

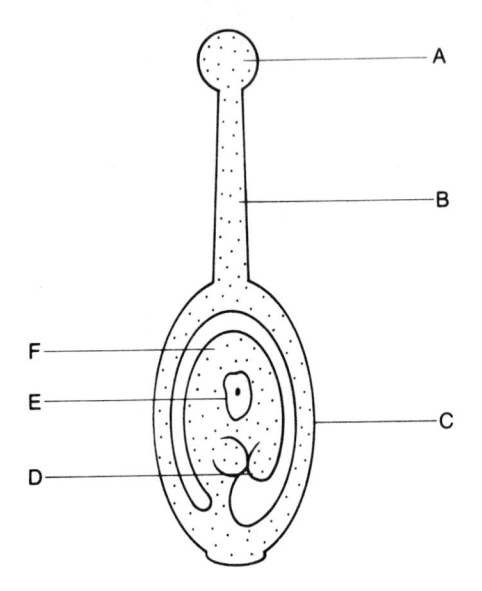

b) Complete the diagram to show how a pollen grain, once it has landed on the stigma, fertilises the ovule.

11 Copy and complete this table to show what happens to the flower parts after fertilisation:

Flower parts	What happens after fertilisation
Petals	wither away
Sepals	
Stamens	
Ovule	
Ovary	

Topic 2 The world of plants

12 Explain each of the following:

  a) Wind-pollinated flowers do not have brightly coloured petals, do not have nectaries and are not scented.

  b) The stamens of wind-pollinated flowers hang outside the petals. The anthers are loosely attached to the filaments.

  c) The stigmas of wind-pollinated flowers are often feathery and hang outside the petals.

  d) The pollen grains of wind-pollinated flowers are very light and are produced in vast numbers.

  e) The pollen grains of insect-pollinated flowers have spikes.

13 The inflorescence of a grass is made up of many small wind-pollinated flowers.

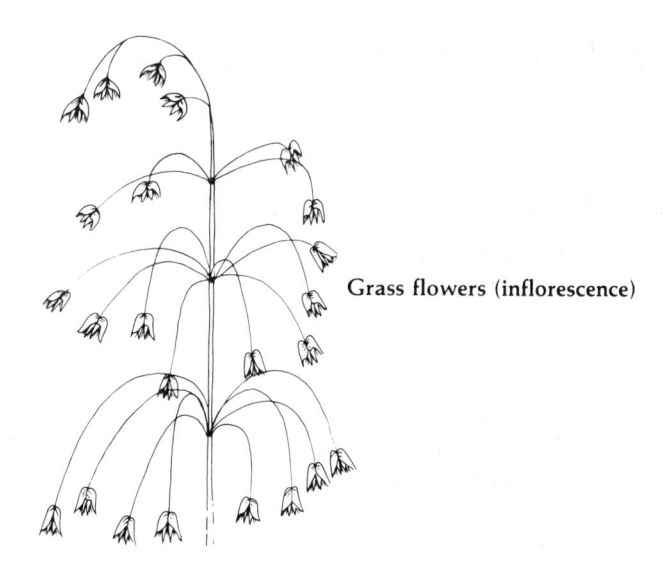

Grass flowers (inflorescence)

  a) What is an inflorescence?

  b) Copy the diagram on the next page of a single grass flower. Replace the letters A to G with labels chosen from this list:

   anther   filament   ovary   pollen grains   stamen   stigma
   style

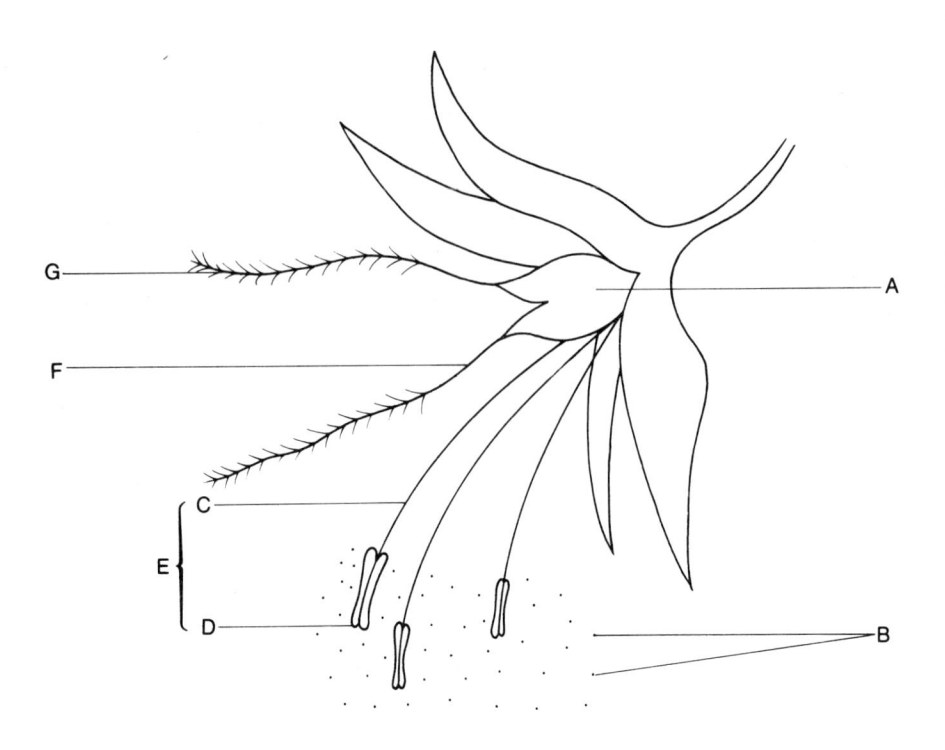

c) What features of this flower help to make wind pollination successful?

14 a) What is meant by seed dispersal?
b) Write down *two* advantages to a plant of having its seeds dispersed away from the parent plant.

15 The following are drawings of fruits. Copy them and next to each one write down an explanation of how seed dispersal is brought about. The dandelion has been done for you as an example.

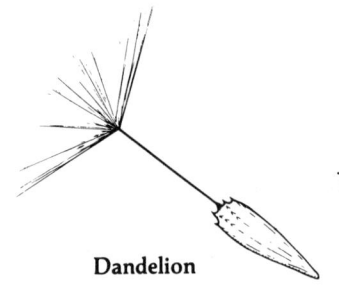

Dandelion

The fruit has a parachute of hairs and is blown about by the wind.

Topic 2 The world of plants

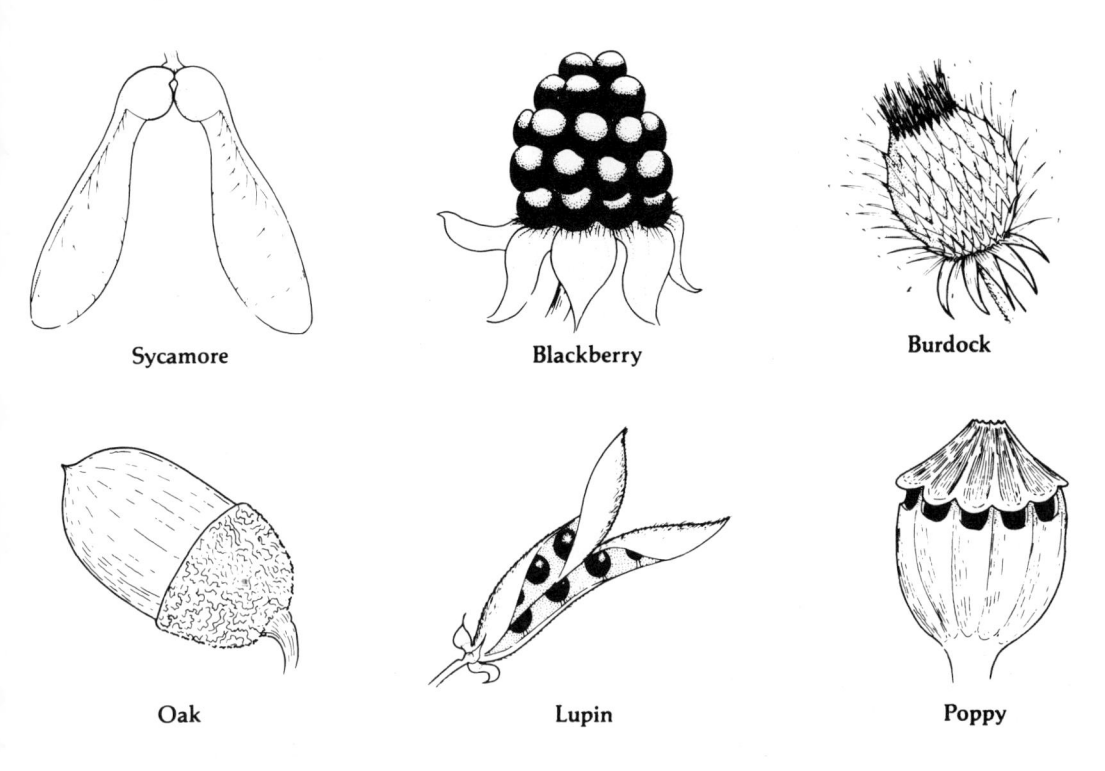

Sycamore

Blackberry

Burdock

Oak

Lupin

Poppy

16 a) By using labelled diagrams, explain how gardeners may reproduce plants by the following methods:

      cuttings   layering   grafting and budding

  b) Why do gardeners carry out the processes of grafting and budding?

  c) What are the advantages of vegetative reproduction

    i) to the plants?

    ii) to the gardener?

  d) What is meant by the term 'clone'?

17 The diagram on the next page shows a plant that produces **runners**. Two young plants are growing from the runner. Strawberry plants spread in this way.

  a) Use diagrams to show how a plant such as the strawberry reproduces by means of runners.

  b) What advantage to the strawberry plant is there in reproducing in this way?

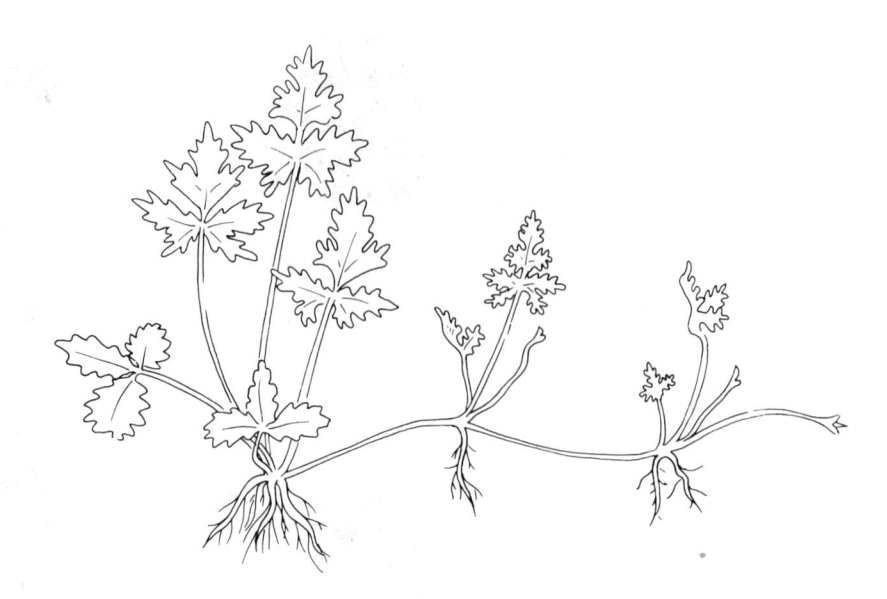

18 a) Why would a gardener choose to grow plants from bulbs rather than from seeds?

b) A man wanted to have a colourful display of flowers in his garden in the spring. Therefore he bought some daffodil, tulip and hyacinth bulbs and planted them in the autumn. The next spring he had a wonderful show of flowers.

Would the man need to plant more bulbs the following autumn to get the same show of flowers the next spring? Explain your answer.

19 Study the diagram (opposite) of a potato plant in July and answer the following questions:

a) Explain why the structure A is in a shrivelled condition at this time of year.

b) Assuming that all the tubers develop, how many new plants will this plant produce in the following spring?

c) What would be likely to develop from structure B?

d) Explain why all the new plants will be identical to the original plant.

e) Food is stored in structure C.

    i) What type of food is stored?

    ii) What chemical test would show the presence of this food?

    iii) Where and how is the stored food made?

    iv) How are the food products transported from the place where they are made to the tubers?

Topic 2 The world of plants

A potato plant in July

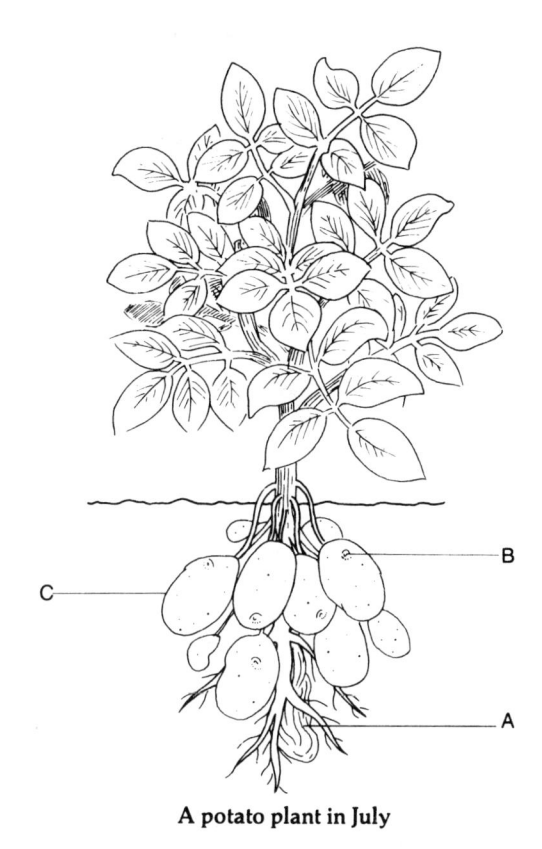

v) What happens to the stored food when the tubers start to develop in the spring?

vi) Why is the potato plant so important to humans?

20 Complete the following sentences by choosing the correct word or words from inside the brackets.

a) Asexual reproduction (involves/does not involve) the production of male and female sex cells.

b) Sexual reproduction (involves/does not involve) the production of male and female sex cells.

c) Offspring produced by asexual reproduction are always (different/identical) and so there is (no/much) variation.

d) Offspring produced by sexual reproduction are always (different/identical) and so there is (no/much) variation.

21 a) Write down *one* advantage and *one* disadvantage of sexual reproduction.

b) Write down *one* advantage and *one* disadvantage of asexual reproduction.

48 Topic 2 The world of plants

3 Making Food

1

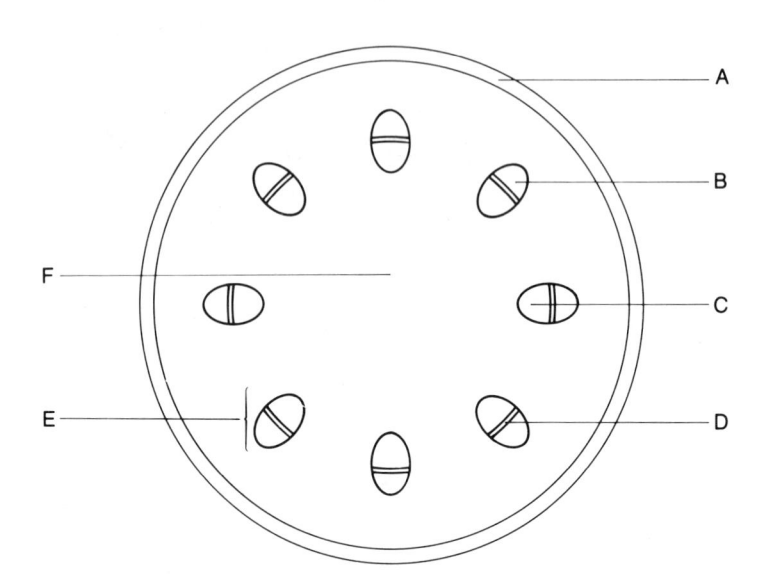

Transverse section of a stem

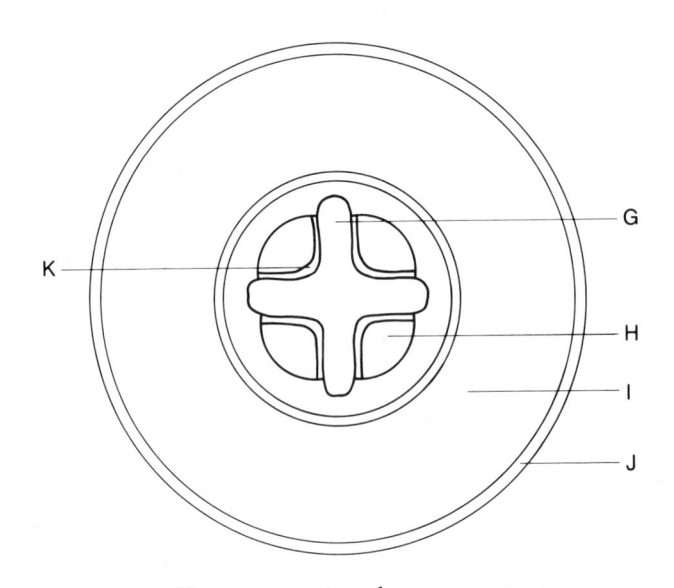

Transverse section of a young root

Topic 2 The world of plants 49

a) Copy the diagrams opposite and replace the letters A to K with the correct tissue name from the list below. (You may use some words more than once.)
cambium   epidermis   packing tissue (parenchyma)   phloem
vascular bundle   xylem

b) Suppose the sections above were taken from a plant that had had its roots placed for at least twelve hours in water containing a red dye. Shade on your drawing the areas that would appear red.

c) What differences can you see between the arrangement of **xylem** and **phloem** in the root and the stem? Suggest the reasons for this. (*Clue words:* support, flexible.)

2 Match the following phrases to make sentences. Each sentence should begin with the phrase on the left and finish with one of the phrases on the right.

a) **The vascular bundles of plants are made up of**   and they contain cytoplasm and sieve plates.

b) **Xylem vessels are dead cells and**   in the sieve tubes of the phloem.

c) **Phloem sieve tubes are living cells**   xylem and phloem tissues.

d) **Water and mineral salts are transported**   their walls are supported by lignin.

e) **Sugars are transported around the plant**   in the xylem vessels.

3 Here are some more phrases to match in the same way:

a) **Evaporation of water from the leaves**   by a waxy cuticle.

b) **The upper surface of leaves is covered**   by the guard cells.

c) **The lower epidermis is pierced**   control the size of the stomatal pores.

d) **The stoma or air pore is surrounded**   by air pores or stomata.

e) **The guard cells**   occurs through stomata.

4 a) Make a large copy of the following diagrams about leaves and their structure:

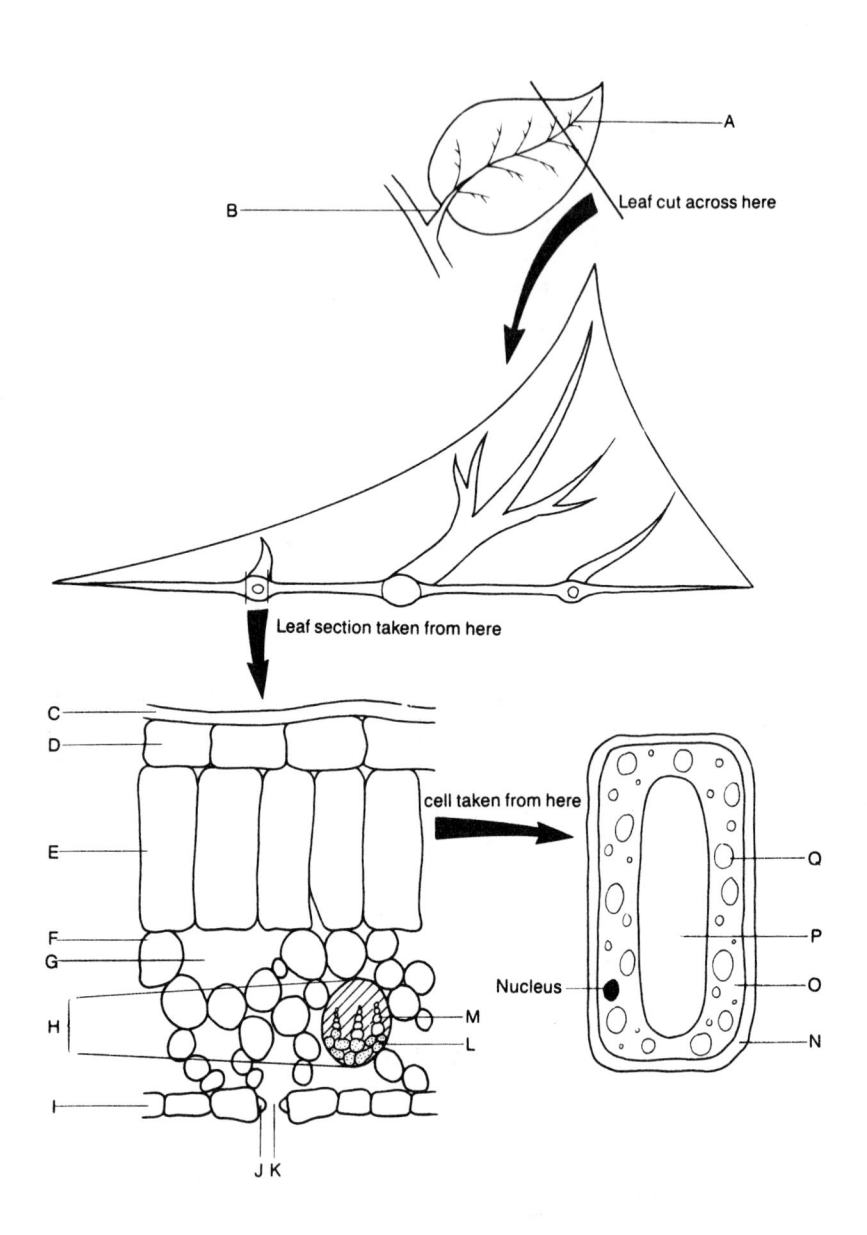

b) Replace the letters A to Q with the correct labels chosen from the list below:

air space   cell wall   chloroplast   cytoplasm   guard cell
lower epidermis   main vein (midrib)   palisade cell
petiole (leaf stalk)   phloem   side vein   spongy mesophyll cell
stomatal pore   upper epidermis   vacuole   waxy cuticle   xylem

Topic 2 The world of plants

5 Complete the following table by suggesting reasons for each of the observations about leaves:

Observation	Reason
Leaves have a large surface area.	
Leaves are often arranged so that they do not shade each other.	
Leaves have stomata.	
Leaves are thin.	
The upper epidermis is covered by a waxy cuticle.	
The mesophyll cells contain chloroplasts.	
The photosynthetic cells are mainly on the upper side of the leaf.	
There are air spaces between the mesophyll cells.	
The leaf contains transport tissue.	
Leaves contain starch.	

6 Three leaves of the same size were cut from a plant. The cut end of each leaf-stalk was sealed. The leaves were then greased in the following way:

> leaf A – the upper surface only was greased
> leaf B – the lower surface only was greased
> leaf C – both surfaces were greased

All leaves were carefully weighed and then suspended in a warm room for six hours. They were then reweighed.

The results are given below:

	Mass immediately after greasing /g	Mass after six hours /g
Leaf A	5	3
Leaf B	5	4.5
Leaf C	6	6

a) For each leaf calculate the percentage loss of mass.

b) Through which surface did the greatest water loss take place?

c) Name and draw the pore, and its surrounding cells, through which water evaporates.

Topic 2 The world of plants

7 An experiment to measure water loss by a potted plant was set up as shown below and left for several days near an open window. The loss in mass was recorded each day and the results are given below.

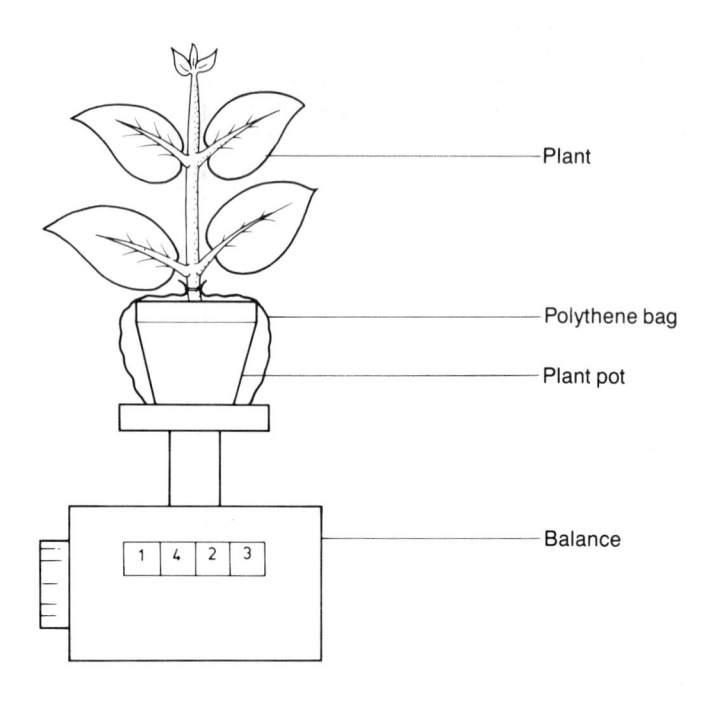

Day	1	2	3	4	5	6	7	8	9	10	11	12
Loss of mass /g	4.2	4.8	5.4	7.0	4.6	8.5	6.0	3.2	4.8	4.6	4.6	4.8

a) Using these results plot a graph to show the amount of water lost each day, putting 'Time /days' on the horizontal axis and 'Mass /g' on the vertical axis.

b) Why was the pot covered with a polythene bag?

c) Using these results, what do you think the weather conditions were likely to have been on

  i) day six?

  ii) day eight?

  Give reasons for your answers.

d) What control would you have used in this experiment?

8 a) Copy and complete the following passage about green plants and the way they feed:

Topic 2 The world of plants

The making of food by green plants is called _____. This process uses _____ energy from the sun. This energy is trapped by the _____ in the leaves. The process also involves two raw materials, _____ from the air and _____ from the soil. Most of the food is made in the _____ of the plant. The most common kind of food they make is _____. Green plants also make the gas _____ during this process.

b) Now complete the following equation, which summarises photosynthesis:

.... + ... ⟶ .... + ...
　　(raw materials)　　　　　　　　　　(products)

c) Copy and complete this diagram by filling in the empty boxes:

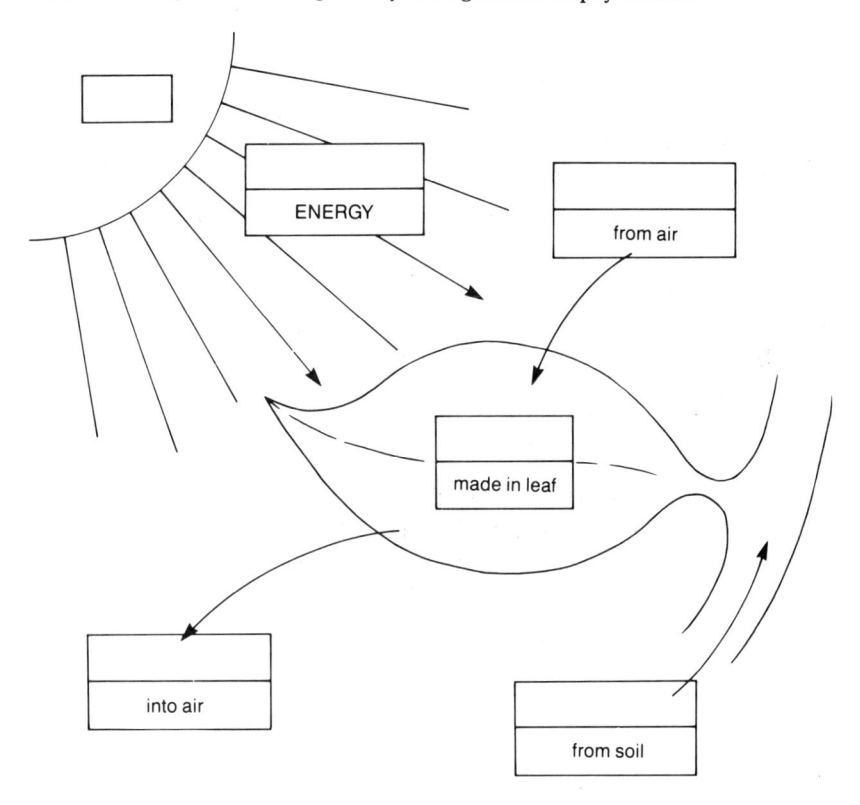

[Diagram with boxes: ENERGY; from air; made in leaf; into air; from soil]

9 a) Match the following pairs of statements and then place them in the correct order in which they occur:

Stages in the starch test	Reason
wash leaf in water	kills leaf
boil leaf in water	softens leaf
cover with iodine solution	removes chlorophyll
boil leaf in ethanol	stains starch

b) What precautions should you take when doing the starch test?
c) What colour will the leaf turn (at the end of the test) if starch is **present**?

10 Study the diagram below and then answer the following questions.

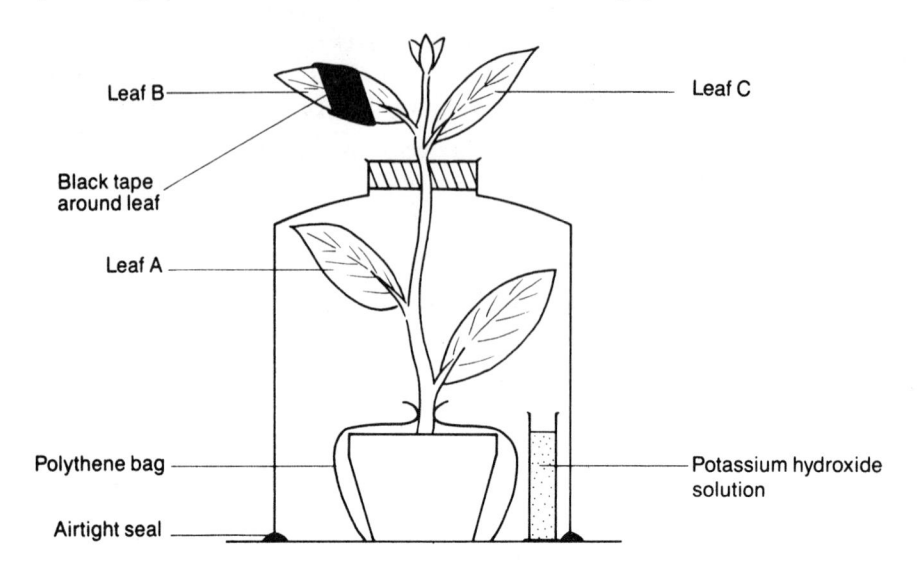

a) The plant was kept in the dark for 24 hours before being placed in sunlight. Why?
b) What is the function of the potassium hydroxide solution?
c) Why is the pot enclosed in a polythene bag?
d) Why is it important to have an airtight seal at the base of the bell jar?
e) The apparatus was set up as in the diagram and left for about twelve hours. Starch tests were carried out on leaf A, leaf B and leaf C. What would you expect the results to be? What do the results tell you about the conditions needed for photosynthesis?
f) Which one is the control leaf and why is it necessary?

11 a) What is unusual about leaf A below?

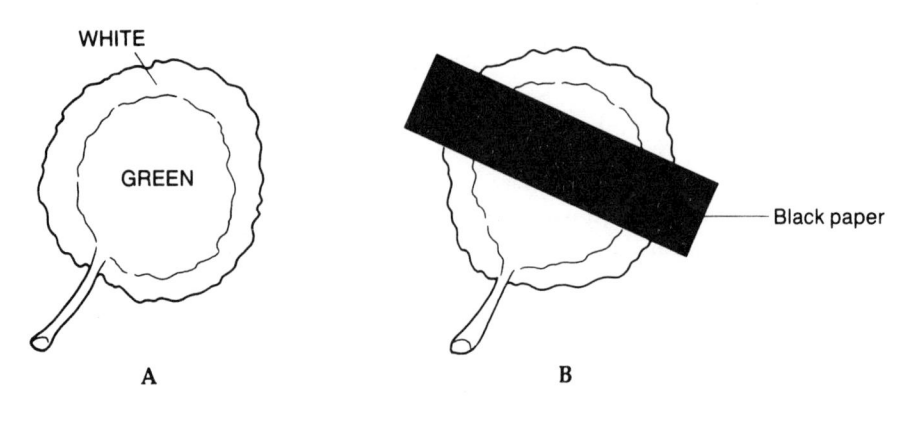

Topic 2 The world of plants

b) How would you remove all the starch from a leaf?

c) Both the leaves opposite were destarched, then exposed to bright sunlight for six hours. If both leaves were then tested for starch in the usual way, what would they look like? Draw a diagram of each leaf to show the result.

d) What have you found out from this experiment?

12 The diagram below shows an experiment that was carried out to measure how fast a water plant such as *Elodea* photosynthesises.

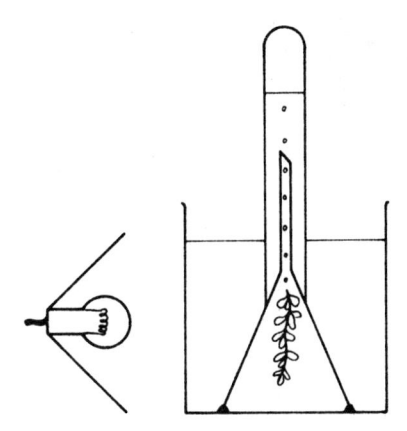

The shoot was exposed to different light intensities and the rate of photosynthesis estimated by counting the number of bubbles of gas leaving the shoot in a given time. The results are given below.

Number of bubbles per minute	7	14	20	24	26	27	27
Light intensity (arbitrary units)	1	2	3	4	5	6	7

a) Plot these data on a piece of graph paper, putting 'Light intensity' on the horizontal axis and 'Number of bubbles' on the vertical axis.

Study the diagram and the graph and then answer the following questions:

b) At what light intensity did the shoot produce 22 bubbles per minute?

c) Can you think of a better way of measuring the rate of photosynthesis than counting the bubbles?

d) What would be the effect of doing this experiment at the following temperatures?

    i)   4 °C   ii)   30 °C   iii) 60 °C

e) What other factor can affect the rate of photosynthesis?

Topic 3

Animal survival

Topic 3 Animal survival

1 The Need for Food

1 Using the following words, write a few sentences to explain why we and all other organisms need food:

   energy   warmth   growth   repair   healthy   movement

2 A balanced diet consists of roughage (or dietary fibre) plus six other substances; what are they?

3 Copy and complete this table by placing a tick under each element that is found in the foods given:

	Carbon	Hydrogen	Oxygen	Nitrogen
Carbohydrate				
Protein				
Fat				

4 Copy and complete these sentences about **carbohydrates**:
   a) Starch, glucose and sucrose and all _____ .
   b) Glucose is a single _____ or **monosaccharide**.
   c) Sucrose is a double sugar or _____ .
   d) Starch is made up of long chains of _____ molecules.
   e) Carbohydrates are needed in the diet to provide _____ .
   f) Examples of foods rich in starch are _____ , _____ and _____ .
   g) Sugar is found in foods such as _____ and _____ .
   h) In the liver, carbohydrate is stored as _____ .

5 Copy and complete this sentences about **proteins**:
   a) Proteins are made up of smaller units called _____ .
   b) About _____ different amino acids occur in nature.
   c) Small chains of amino acids are called _____ .

Topic 3 Animal survival 59

d) Some proteins are tough and fibre-like, forming structures such as hair, _____ and _____ .

e) Substances called _____ are proteins that control reactions in cells.

f) Good sources of protein in the diet are _____ , _____ and _____ .

g) Protein in the diet is needed for _____ and _____ .

6 Copy and complete these sentences about **fats**:

a) Fats are made up of smaller units called _____ and _____ .

b) Different kinds of fats contain different _____ .

c) One function of fat is to give us _____ .

d) Many fats provide a source of fat-soluble _____ .

e) Fat stored under the skin _____ the body.

f) Good sources of fat in the diet are _____ and _____ .

g) It is healthier to use vegetable _____ rather than animal fat.

7 In the early 1900s Sir Frederick Gowland Hopkins performed experiments on rats and their diet. In one experiment he divided some rats from the same litter into two groups. Group A were fed on purified cheese protein, glucose, starch, lard, minerals and water. Group B received exactly the same food plus 3 cm^3 of milk per day. After 18 days Group A instead of Group B were given the milk. The results are shown below.

Time /days	Average mass of rats in Group A /g	Average mass of rats in Group B /g
0	45	45
5	48	55
10	52	64
15	50	73
20	46	80
25	50	85
30	60	86
35	65	87
40	70	87
45	76	82
50	82	75

Plot the results on a graph, putting 'Time /days' on the horizontal axis. Above day 18 draw a vertical dotted line to show where the diets were changed.

Now study your graph and try to answer these questions:

a) Why did Gowland Hopkins use two groups of rats rather than two individuals?

b) Why did he use rats that all came from the same litter?

c) What was the average mass of rats in Groups A and B on day 18?

d) On which days were the masses of Groups A and B equal?

e) After the change of diet on day 18 what happened to Group B's mass and why?

f) After the change of diet on day 18 why did the mass of Group A not rise immediately?

g) Why did Gowland Hopkins change the diets over?

h) Other than milk, why was it important that both Groups of rats should receive equal amounts of food and water?

i) If the experiment had been continued for a further 20 days what do you think would have happened to the masses of Groups A and B?

j) What conclusions do you think Gowland Hopkins came to after seeing the results of this experiment?

> *Did You Know?*
> The use of food additives is so widespread that the average person probably consumes about five kilograms in a year.

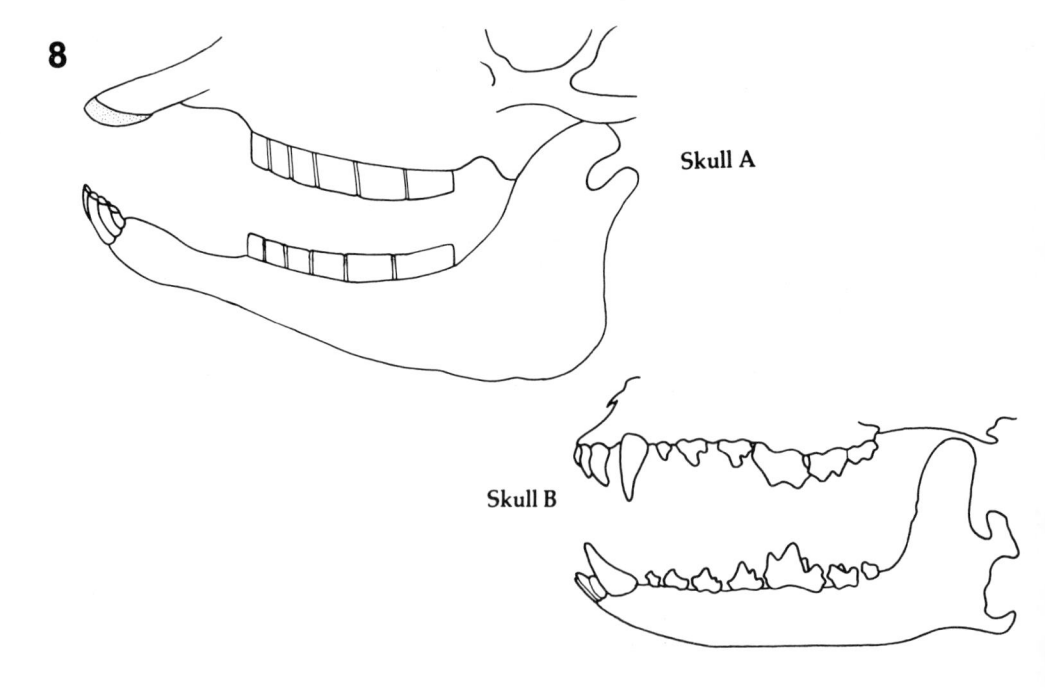

8

Skull A

Skull B

a) Study the diagrams above of the two skulls A and B, and then complete the following table by using the words 'yes' or 'no':

Topic 3   Animal survival

	Skull A	Skull B
Does the animal eat plant matter (is a herbivore)?		
Does the animal eat other animals (is a carnivore)?		
Is there a gap between the front and back teeth for holding food?		
Are the upper incisors replaced by a hard pad?		
Are the canines missing or reduced in size?		
Are the canines large and dagger-like?		
Are the cheek teeth jagged?		
Do the cheek teeth have a flat grinding surface?		

b) Name *four* plant-eating animals that have cheek teeth similar to those in skull A.

c) Name *four* meat-eating animals that have large canines similar to those in skull B.

d) What does the word 'omnivorous' mean? Name *two* omnivorous animals.

e) Now copy the diagram of skull A and underneath it write a few sentences describing how this animal uses its teeth and jaws to feed. Then do the same for skull B.

9 Copy and complete the following table about human teeth:

Name of tooth	Diagram of shape of tooth	Main function
Incisor		
Premolar		
Canine		
Molar		

10 The diagrams below show plans of teeth in the upper and lower jaw.

Plan A belongs to a 25-year-old man called Mike.
Plan B belongs to a 25-year-old man called Peter.

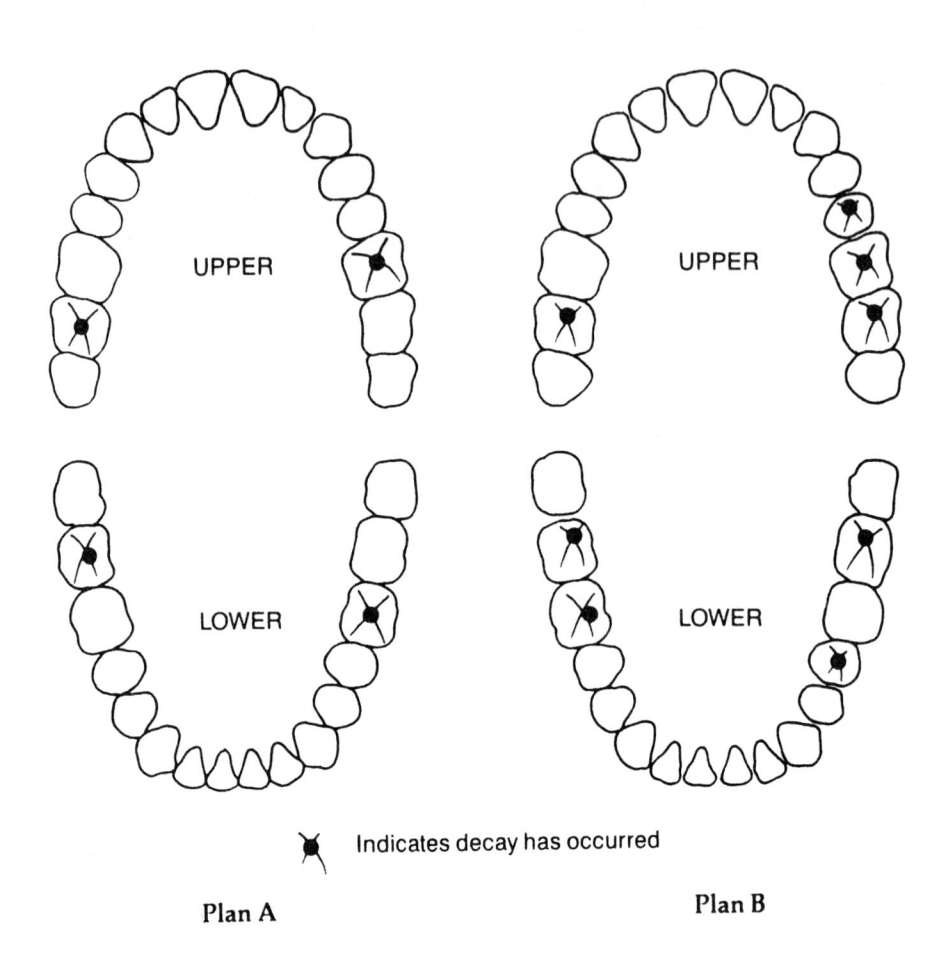

✖ Indicates decay has occurred

Plan A   Plan B

a) In which type of tooth has most decay occurred? Suggest a reason for this.
b) How many decayed teeth has
   i) Mike?
   ii) Peter?
c) What is the percentage of decayed teeth in
   i) Mike?
   ii) Peter?
d) Suggest three possible reasons why Peter has more decayed teeth than Mike.

Topic 3 Animal survival

11

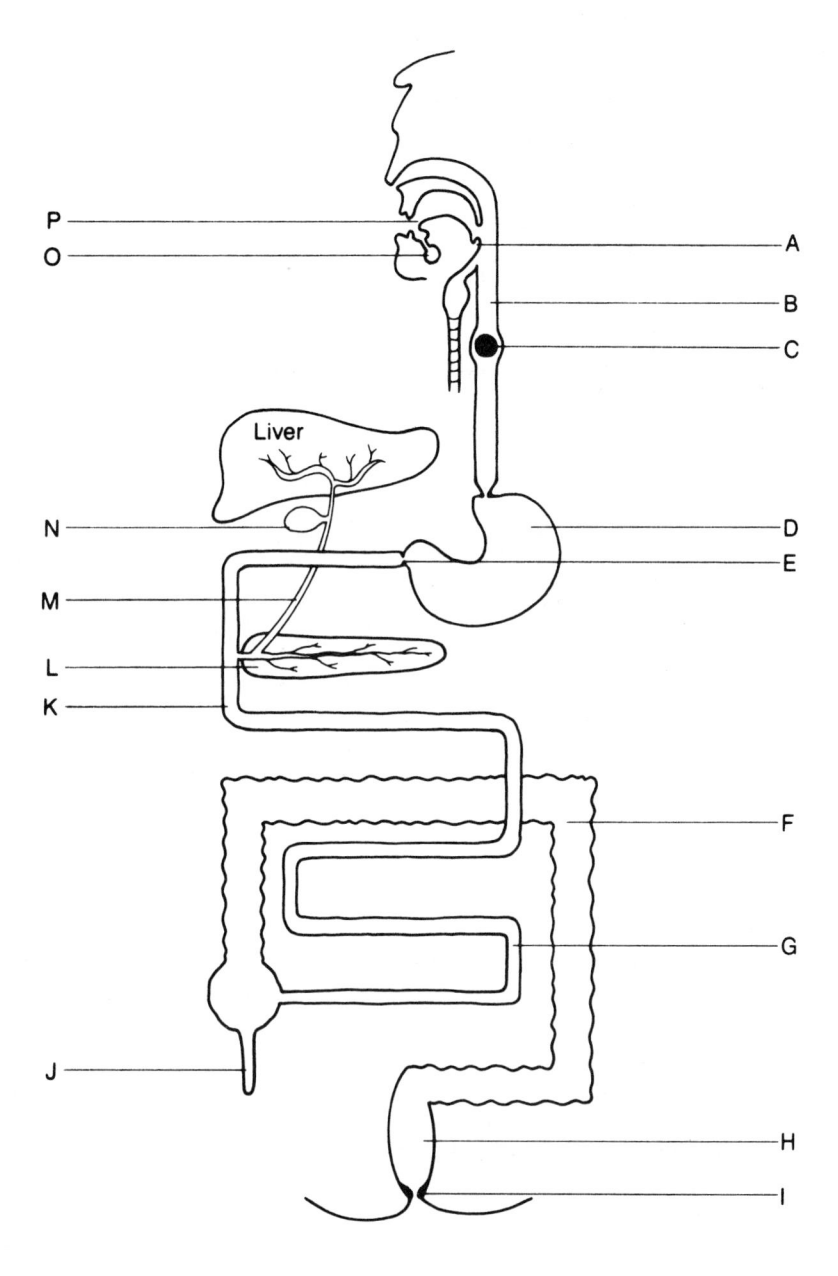

Copy the above diagram, which represents the human gut. Replace the letters A–P with the correct labels chosen from the list provided:

anus   appendix   bile duct   bolus of food   colon   duodenum
epiglottis   gall bladder   ileum   mouth   oesphagus   pancreas
pyloric sphincter muscle   rectum   salivary gland   stomach

> *Did You Know?*
> The human gut is approximately 8 metres long.

12 From the two lists below match each structure with its correct function. (The first one has been done for you as an example.)

Salivary glands ... produce saliva

Structure	Function
Salivary glands	produces enzymes which pass into the duodenum
The oesophagus	controls the passing of faeces
The stomach	produce saliva
The pyloric sphincter muscle	is where most water is absorbed
The duodenum	carries food from the mouth to the stomach
The ileum	stores bile
The bile duct	receives juices from the gall bladder and pancreas
The pancreas	controls the amount of food leaving the stomach
The gall bladder	stores waste faeces for several hours
The colon	produces hydrochloric acid
The rectum	is where most digested food is absorbed
The anus	takes bile from the gall bladder to the duodenum

13 Complete these sentences about what happens in the gut, by filling in the missing words:

An egg sandwich contains starch, fat and protein: the starch is in the _____, most of the fat is in the _____ and much of the protein is in the _____. When this sandwich enters your _____ it is chopped up into small pieces by your teeth. This increases the _____ of the food so that the digestive enzymes of the gut can act more quickly. These enzymes break the food down even more, changing _____ molecules like starch into _____ soluble molecules such as glucose. These soluble molecules can pass through the lining of the gut into the _____.

14 Answer the following questions about the way we digest our food:
   a) Saliva contains water together with two other important substances. What are they?
   b) What are the main functions of saliva?
   c) How is solid food moved down the gullet (oesophagus)?
   d) What is this process called?

Topic 3 Animal survival

e) What structure prevents food from entering the windpipe?

f) Name one digestive enzyme produced by the stomach wall, and the type of food substance it helps to break up?

g) The stomach also produces acid. What is this acid for?

h) How is the stomach wall protected from the acid?

i) How does the muscle in the wall of the stomach help digestion?

j) The digestive enzymes of the small intestine work best in alkaline conditions; how, therefore, is the acid from the stomach neutralised?

k) Where is bile

  i) made?

  ii) stored?

  iii) mixed with food?

l) What does bile do?

m) The pancreas produces a juice which contains three important enzymes; name the enzyme which acts upon

  i) starch

  ii) protein

  iii) fat

n) Why must food be digested before it can be absorbed?

o) Give *two* ways in which the wall of the small intestine is adapted to absorb digested food.

p) As a result of digestion what are the following foods finally broken down into:

  i) starch

  ii) protein

  iii) fat

q) Why is roughage (or dietary fibre) important in the human diet?

Did You Know?
The record for constipation is 102 days.

15 Copy and complete the following table to show where starch, protein and fat are digested in the human gut. Put ticks in the correct boxes. (The first one has been done for you as an example.)

	Starch	Protein	Fat
Mouth	✓	—	—
Oesophagus			
Stomach			
Small intestine			
Large intestine			

16 Copy and complete the following table by filling in the blank spaces:

Enzymes	Where produced	Where mixed with food	Food acted on (substrate)	Substances produced (products)
		mouth		maltose
Pepsin				polypeptides
	pancreas		starch	
Lipase				
			proteins and polypeptides	

17 a) Study the details of the experiment described below, and then complete the table by filling in the results that would be expected in each test-tube.

Three mixtures contained in test-tubes were set up as follows:
Tube A: 1% starch solution plus amylase at 37 °C
Tube B: 1% starch solution plus boiled amylase at 37 °C
Tube C: 1% starch solution plus acid plus amylase at 37 °C

After twenty minutes, samples from each tube were tested with iodine solution and Benedict's reagent.

Did You Know?
Every day we secrete about 1 litre of saliva.

Topic 3 Animal survival

	Colour of Tube A	Colour of Tube B	Colour of Tube C
Tested with iodine solution			
Tested with Benedict's reagent			

b) Where would you find amylase being secreted in the human digestive system?

c) Why are the tubes kept at 37 °C?

d) Where are the conditions found in Tube C likely to occur in the human digestive system?

18 The detailed structure of the wall of the small intestine reveals many features that make it well suited to the digestion and absorption of food.

From the diagrams below, list as many of these features as you can, under these two headings:

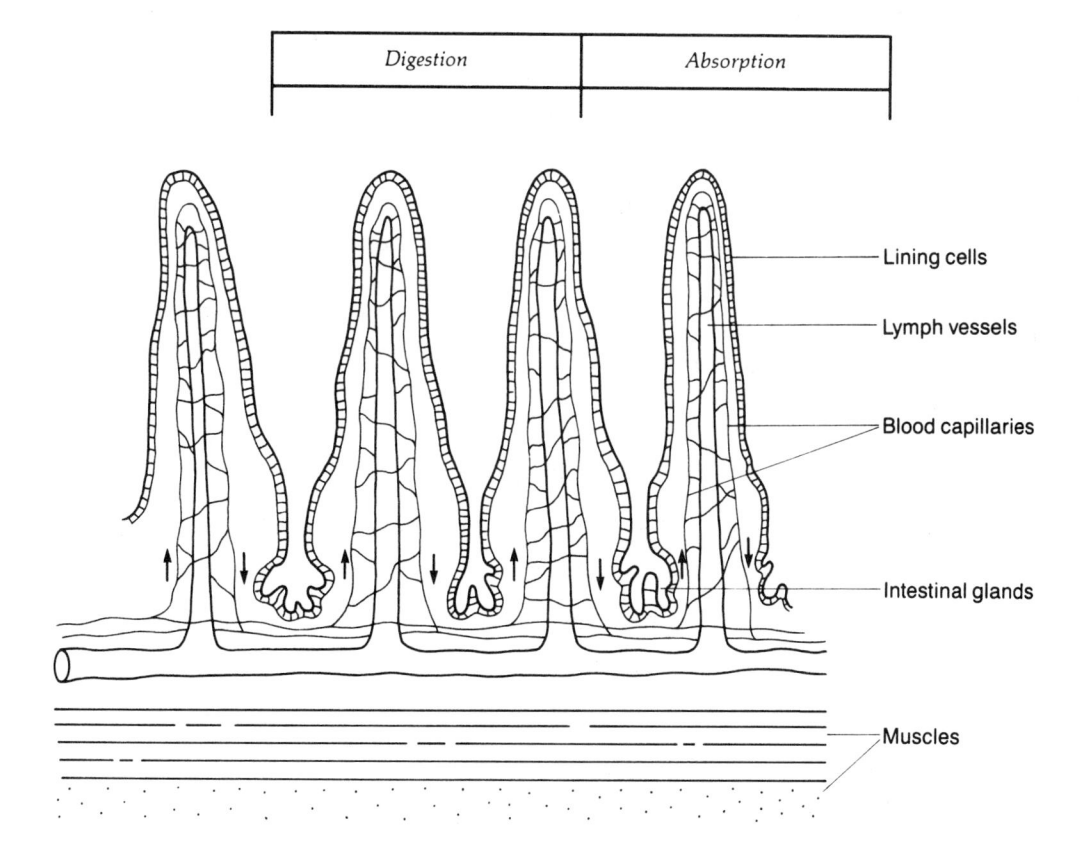

Digestion	Absorption

Labels on diagram: Lining cells, Lymph vessels, Blood capillaries, Intestinal glands, Muscles

2 Reproduction

1 Complete this diagram:

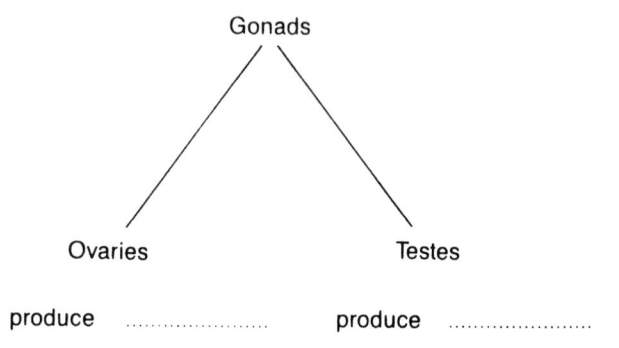

```
              Gonads
             /      \
            /        \
           /          \
        Ovaries      Testes

        produce  ............   produce  ............
```

2 Use labelled diagrams to show the structure of a human egg and a human sperm.

3 Write down *four* ways in which an egg differs from a sperm. (*Clue words*: shape, size, food, movement.)

4 Use labelled diagrams to show how **fertilisation** takes place.

5 Explain the difference between internal fertilisation in a mammal and external fertilisation in a fish.

6 Match each of the following with one of the definitions below:

        gamete   **egg**   **sperm**   **fertilisation**   **zygote**   **embryo**

a) Male sex cell

b) The joining of male and female sex cells

c) A fertilised egg develops into this

d) Female sex cell

e) The biological name for a sex cell

f) A fertilised egg

Topic 3 Animal survival

7 Copy this diagram of the human **male reproductive system**. Replace the letters A to E with labels chosen from this list:

penis   scrotum   sperm duct   testis   urethra

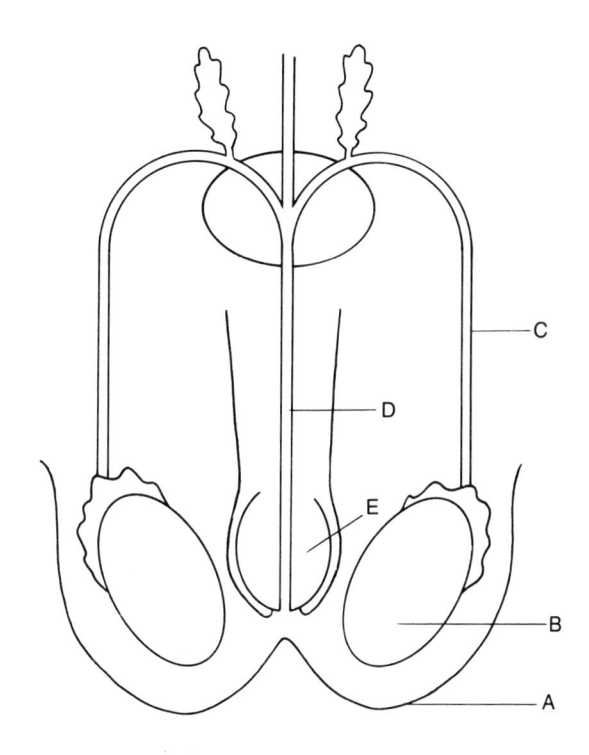

Did You Know?
There are over a kilometre of sperm-producing tubes in each testis.

8 Using the descriptions (a–i) below, write a couple of sentences about each of the following organs of the male reproductive system:

testes   scrotum   penis   sperm ducts

a) There are two of them.
b) It is the loose sac of skin that contains the testes.
c) They connect the testes to the urethra.
d) The urethra runs though this organ.
e) It contains large numbers of blood vessels.

f) The organs in which sperms are made.

g) They are suspended in the scrotal sac.

h) It becomes erect during intercourse.

i) They are made up of a large number of tiny tubules.

> *Did You Know?*
> The average adult male produces approximately 300 million sperms each day.

9 Copy this diagram of the human **female reproductive system**. Replace the letters A to F with labels chosen from this list:

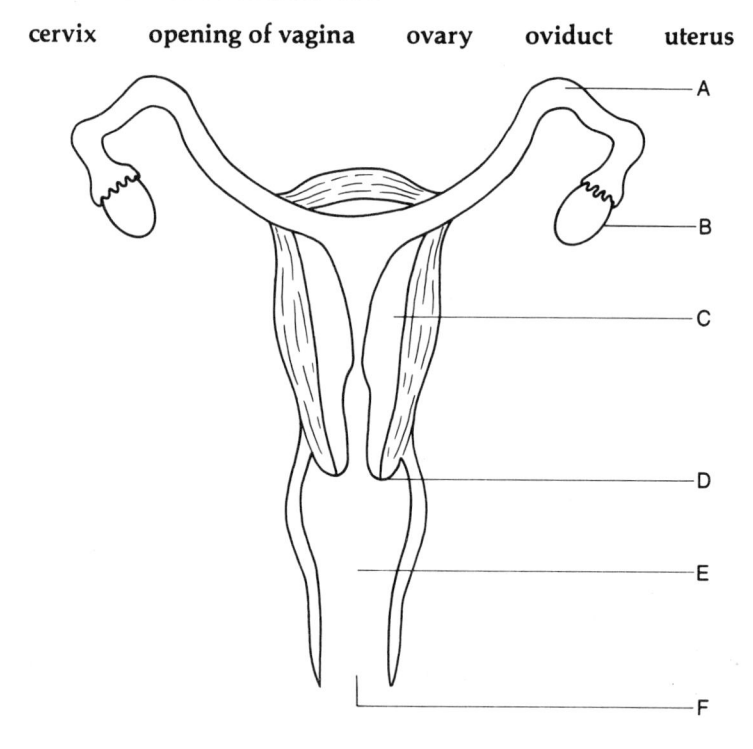

cervix   opening of vagina   ovary   oviduct   uterus   vagina

10 Mark on your diagram of the female reproductive system
   a) where fertilisation occurs
   b) where implantation occurs
   c) where sperms are deposited during intercourse

Topic 3 Animal survival

11 Write down these names of organs of the female reproductive system:

   ovaries   oviducts   uterus   cervix   vagina

   Below each one, write down the correct descriptions of the organ from the following list:

   a) The neck of the uterus.
   b) Its common name is the womb.
   c) There is one on each side of the abdomen.
   d) It connects the uterus to the exterior.
   e) They connect the ovaries to the uterus.
   f) The organs in which eggs are produced.
   g) A pear-shaped organ with a muscular wall.
   h) The place where fertilisation occurs.
   i) The place where sperms are deposited during intercourse.
   j) They are also called the Fallopian tubes.
   k) The place where the baby develops.
   l) One egg is released from here about every 28 days.

12 Correctly match the words in the left-hand column with the definitions in the right-hand column.

Words	Definitions
ovulation	the release of semen from the penis
semen	the release of an egg from an ovary
ejaculation	the sinking of a fertilised egg into the lining of the uterus
fertilisation	the fluid containing sperms
implantation	the joining of an egg with a sperm

13 Complete the following sentences, choosing the best word or words from those in the lists:

   a) Pregnancy begins when . . .
      i) an egg is released from the ovary.
      ii) intercourse takes place.
      iii) an egg is fertilised.
      iv) a fertilised egg sinks into the lining of the uterus.

b) A baby develops inside the . . .
   i) Fallopian tube.
   ii) ovary.
   iii) uterus (womb).
   iv) vagina.

c) The foetus is surrounded by a thin membrane called the . . .
   i) amnion.
   ii) placenta.
   iii) umbilicus.
   iv) uterus.

d) The foetus is cushioned by the . . .
   i) placenta.
   ii) mother's blood.
   iii) amniotic fluid.
   iv) umbilical cord.

e) The foetus gets its food and oxygen from the mother's blood through the . . .
   i) amnion.
   ii) embryo.
   iii) amnionic fluid.
   iv) placenta.

f) The waste products that pass from the foetus into the mother's blood include . . .
   i) oxygen and urea.
   ii) faeces and urea.
   iii) carbon dioxide and urea.

g) Conception is the time when . . .
   i) an egg is released.
   ii) an egg is fertilised.
   iii) an embryo becomes a foetus.

Topic 3 Animal survival

14 Copy the diagrams below. Replace the letters A to H on both diagrams with labels from this list:

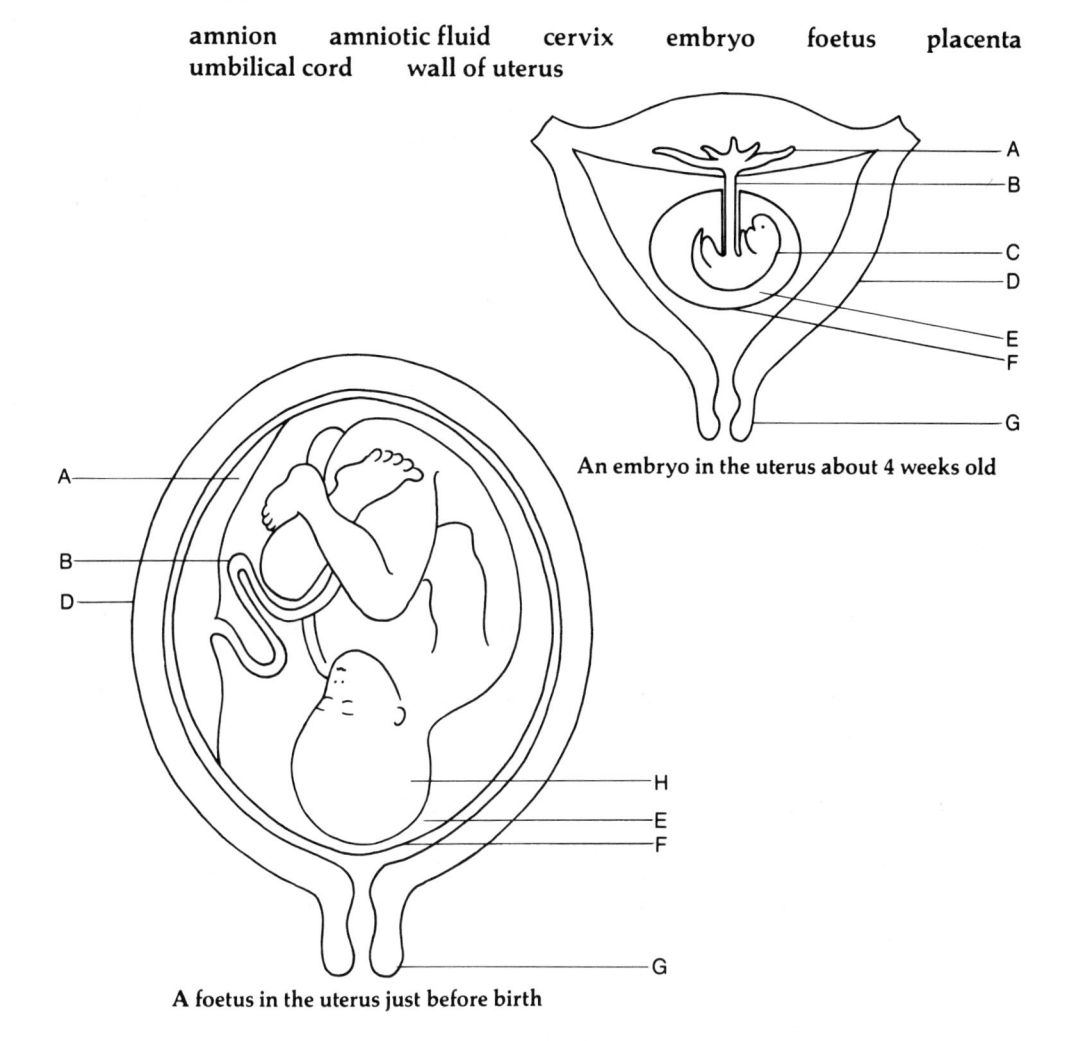

   amnion   amniotic fluid   cervix   embryo   foetus   placenta
   umbilical cord   wall of uterus

An embryo in the uterus about 4 weeks old

A foetus in the uterus just before birth

15 Some information on the growth of a human baby *before* birth is given in the table below.

Age /months	0	1	2	3	4	5	6	7	8	9
Length /cm	0	1	4	9	16	25	30	34	38	42

a) Draw the growth curve from this information.

b) When is the baby growing

  i) most rapidly?

  ii) most slowly?

16 Look carefully at this diagram, which shows the relationship between the blood system of the foetus and that of the mother, and then answer the questions:

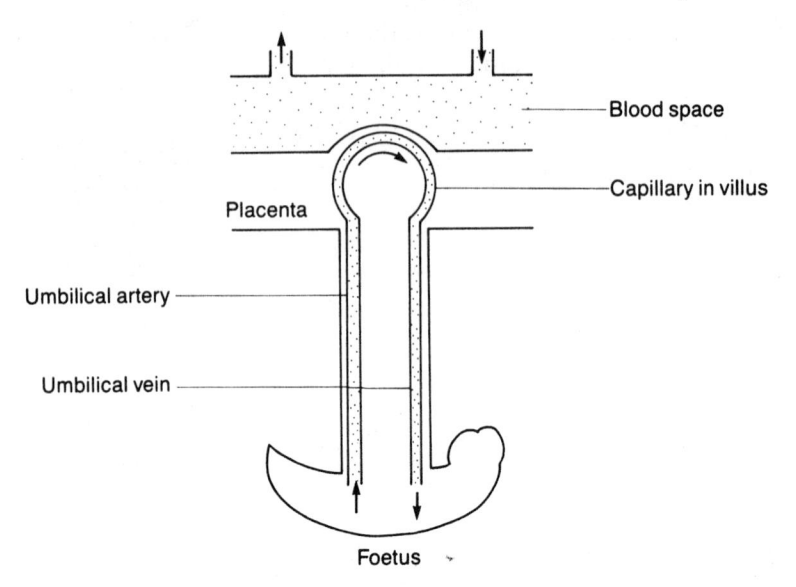

a) Which blood vessel carries blood, rich in waste products, from the foetus to the placenta?

b) Which blood vessel carries blood, rich in food and oxygen, from the placenta to the foetus?

17 Study this table and then answer the questions:

Animal	Number of eggs produced per year	Where eggs are laid
Cod	9 000 000	water
Frog	10 000	water
Turtle	1000	sand
Penguin	8	land

a) Write down *two* reasons why fish lay so many eggs.

b) Why does a frog lay fewer eggs than a cod, even though they both lay their eggs in water?

c) Why do penguins lay fewer eggs than turtles?

18 Babies require only milk for the first few weeks of their life.

a) What are the advantages of breast-feeding?

b) What is the name of the glands in the breasts which secrete the milk?

c) How are babies provided with food before they are born?

Topic 3 Animal survival

   d) From where does a young fish get its food
      i) before it is born?
      ii) after it is born?
   e) In what ways, other than for food, are young mammals dependent on their parents after they are born?

3 Water and Waste

1 a) Make a *large* copy of the following diagram:

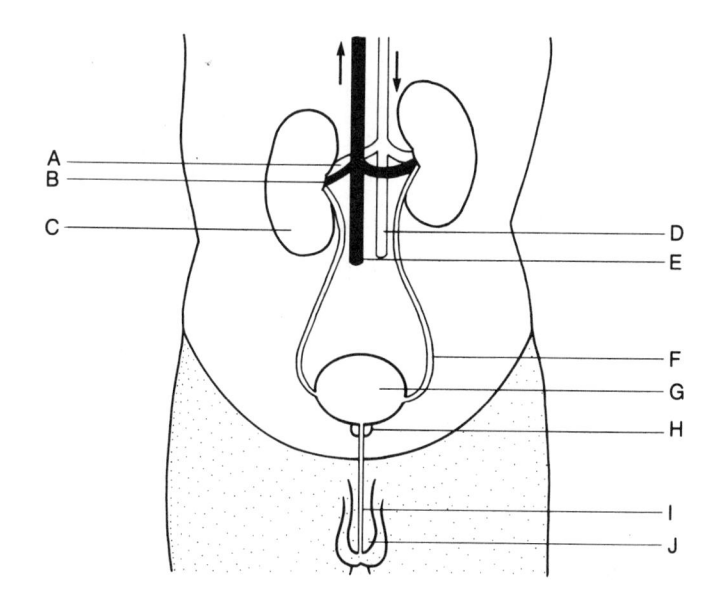

b) Replace the letters A to J with the correct labels chosen from the list below.

   aorta   bladder   kidney   penis   renal artery   renal vein
   ring of muscle   ureter   urethra   vena cava

2 Now make a list of the above labels and for each one choose the correct function from the list (a–g) below.
   a) takes urine from the kidney to the bladder
   b) prevents urine leaving the bladder
   c) carries deoxygenated blood to the heart

d) removes urea from the blood
e) carries urine out of the body
f) also used during sexual intercourse
g) carries blood to the kidney
h) stores urine
i) carries blood away from the kidney
j) brings oxygenated blood from the heart

3 a) Copy this diagram of a section through the kidney:

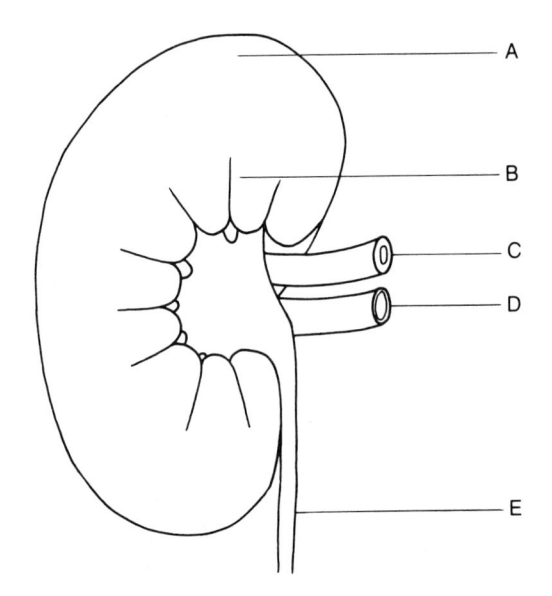

b) Replace the letters A–E with the correct label chosen from the list below.

cortex   medulla   renal artery   renal vein   ureter

4 Complete this passage about the structure of the kidney by filling in the missing words:

The kidney is composed of two main regions, the outer _____ and an inner _____. Under a _____ many tiny nephrons can be seen: there are about one million in each kidney. Each nephron has a cup-shaped capsule at one end. This surrounds a small bunch of _____ called the _____. Leading away from each capsule is a narrow _____ which twists and turns. This eventually joins a collecting _____. These all lead to the _____, which takes urine from the kidney to the _____.

Topic 3 Animal survival

5 Copy the following simplified diagram of a kidney nephron and its blood supply. Explain what happens at each of the stages A to F, which show very simply how the nephron cleans the blood and makes urine.

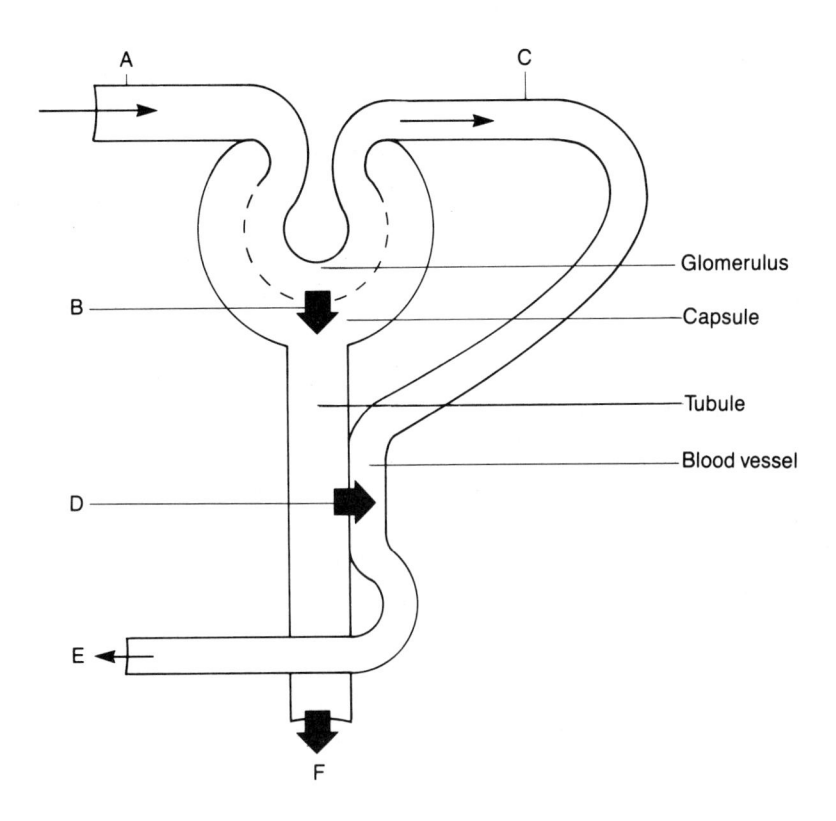

Now try to answer these questions (a–g) as fully as you can:

a) Name the blood vessel that brings blood under high pressure to the kidney.

b) How is high blood pressure produced in the glomerulus?

c) What causes the fluid part of the blood to be forced through the walls of the capillaries into the space inside the capsule?

d) Which of the following
   i) pass through the capillary walls?
   ii) are too large to pass through the capillary walls and so stay in the blood?

   red blood cells   glucose   haemoglobin   urea   protein
   water   salt   white blood cells

e) As the fluid trickles along the tubule, all the glucose and some of the water and salt is taken back (reabsorbed) into the blood. Why is it important that this happens?

f) During some early work on diabetes it was noticed that ants were attracted to the urine of diabetic dogs. What was unusual about the dogs' urine? Doctors used to taste the urine of patients who were suspected of having diabetes. Why did they do this?

g) What is the main toxic or poisonous waste substance found in urine?

6 a) Copy the table below, and complete it with a tick for each substance present and a cross for each substance not present in a normal healthy person.

	Protein	Glucose	Urea	Water	Salt
Blood in renal artery					
Blood in glomerulus					
Fluid that passes into the capsule					
Urine leaving the kidney					
Blood in the renal vein					

b) Give *three* ways in which the blood leaving the kidney will be different from that which entered the kidney.

7 The diagram shows part of an artificial kidney machine.

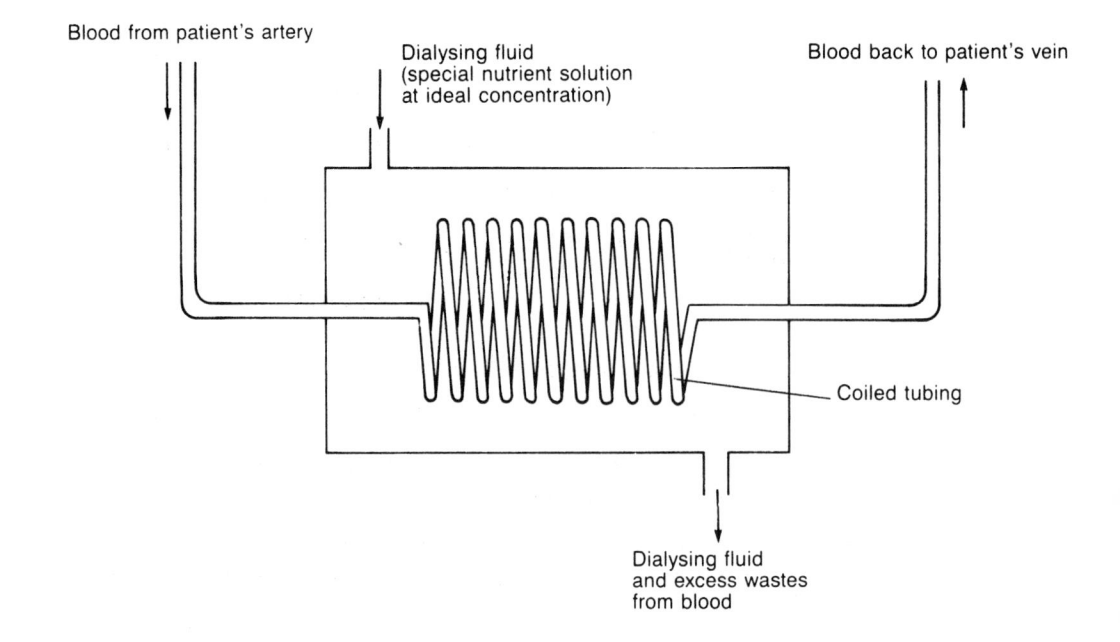

Topic 3 Animal survival 79

    a) Why is the tubing coiled and not straight?

    b) What material is the tubing likely to be made of?

    c) Name an excretory product which will pass out of the blood, with water, into the dialysing fluid.

    d) Where in the body is this excretory product made?

    e) Name two nutrients present in the dialysing fluid.

    f) Give two reasons why kidney transplantation is a better way of treating kidney failure than the use of a dialysis machine.

8 a) Complete this passage by choosing the correct word or words from inside the brackets:

After drinking several cups of tea or coffee the volume of the urine (increases/decreases) and it looks (paler/yellower). The kidney is getting rid of excess (water/salt). On the other hand, on a hot day or after severe exercise the volume of urine (increases/decreases) and it looks (paler/yellower). This is called (excretion/osmoregulation).

    b) Patients requiring dialysis by an artificial kidney machine must restrict their water and salt intake between dialysis sessions. Explain why.

4 Responding to the Environment

1 a) The diagram below shows a vertical section through a piece of apparatus which can be used to investigate the conditions wood-lice prefer.

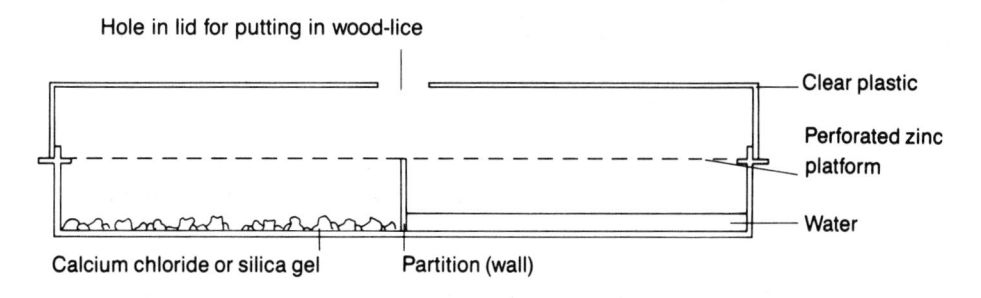

    i) What is the name of this apparatus?

    ii) What is the function of the calcium chloride or silica gel?

(cont.)

Topic 3 Animal survival

b) Ten wood-lice were placed in the apparatus, and the number of wood-lice in each half was counted every minute for six minutes. The results are shown in the table below.

Time/minutes	Number of wood-lice in left-hand side	Number of wood-lice in right-hand side
1	4	6
2	2	8
3	1	9
4	2	8
5	1	9
6	1	9

i) Plot both sets of results on one graph, clearly labelling which curve is which. Label the axes as shown.

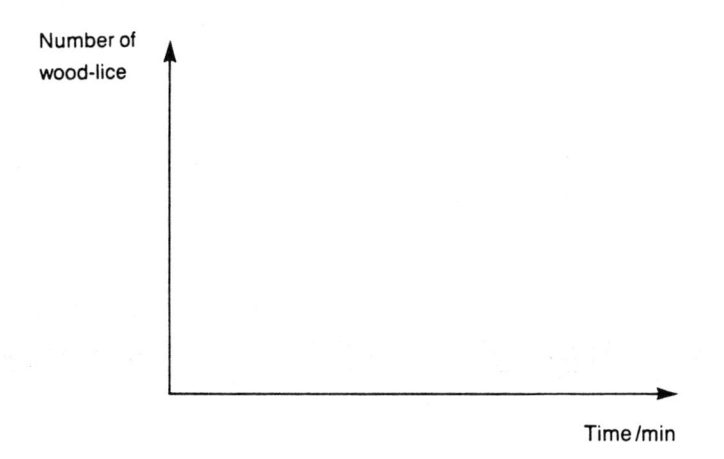

Number of wood-lice

Time/min

ii) Which conditions do the wood-lice prefer?

iii) When the passage between the two sides of the apparatus was blocked, the wood-lice in the dry side were bunched up together against the sides. How does this behaviour help the wood-lice to survive?

c) i) Describe how you could use the same apparatus to see if wood-lice prefer dark or light conditions.

ii) When such an experiment was carried out, it was found that wood-lice preferred the dark conditions. How does this help them to survive?

2 A pupil designed the following experiment to investigate the effect of light on the behaviour of the small freshwater crustacean *Daphnia*.

The tube was gently shaken until the *Daphnia* were evenly distributed in the water (Diagram A).

Topic 3 Animal survival 81

Diagram B shows the re-distribution of the *Daphnia* after several minutes.

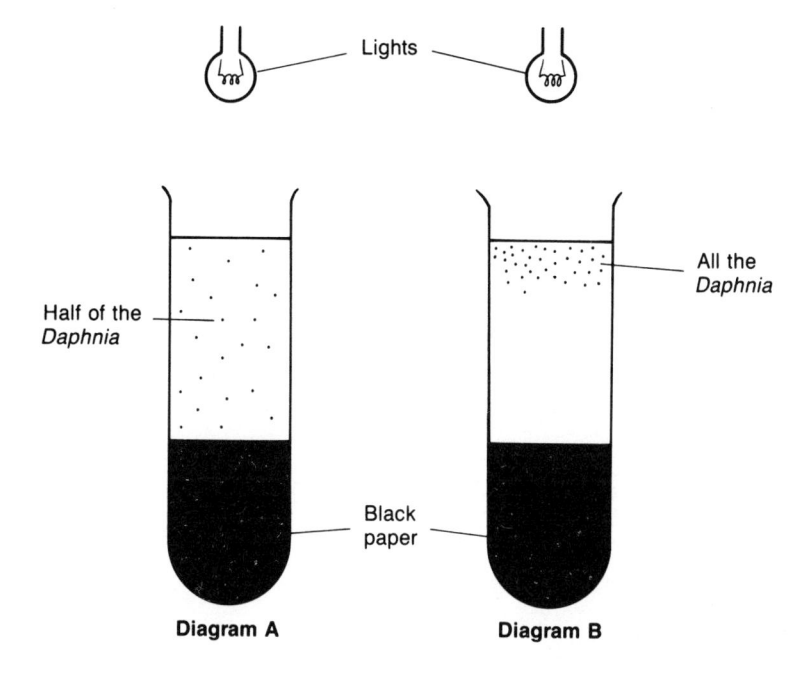

Diagram A — Half of the *Daphnia*, Black paper
Diagram B — All the *Daphnia*

From the above results, the pupil concluded that the *Daphnia* moved towards light.

a) State *two* ways in which the design of the experiment could have been extended to support his conclusion.

b) Suggest *one* other possible hypothesis to account for the distribution of *Daphnia* in Diagram B.

[Scottish Examination Board]

Topic 4

Investigating cells

1 The Structure of Cells

1 This diagram shows the main parts of a typical **light microscope**.

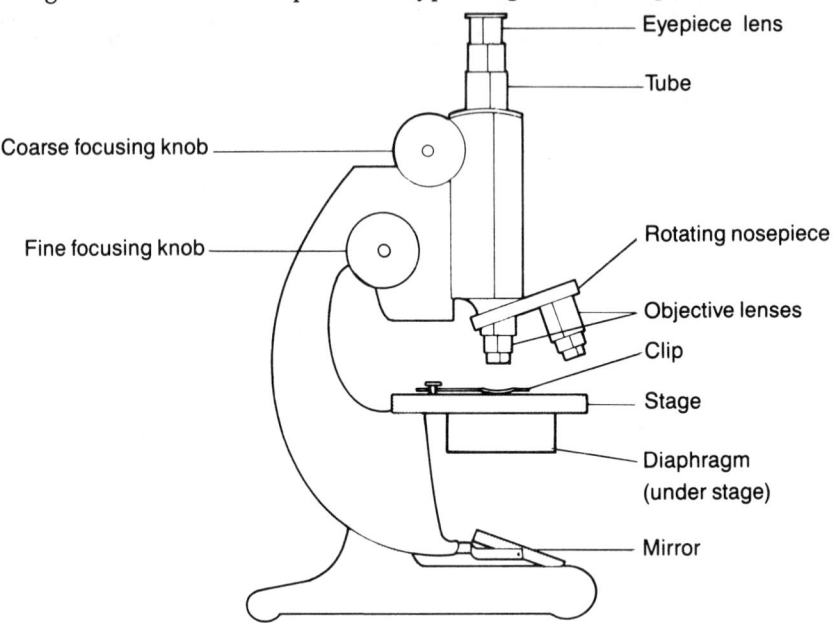

- Eyepiece lens
- Tube
- Coarse focusing knob
- Fine focusing knob
- Rotating nosepiece
- Objective lenses
- Clip
- Stage
- Diaphragm (under stage)
- Mirror

Answer the following questions about how to use this type of microscope.

a) How is a glass slide held in position on the stage?

b) Why must the specimen on the slide be in the centre of the hole in the stage?

c) Why does the nosepiece rotate?

d) What is the mirror for?

e) How can you control the amount of light coming through the microscope?

f) Explain how you would use the microscope to look at a specimen under low power.

g) If you had a specimen in focus under low power, how would you go on to look at it under high power?

h) Why should you never rack downwards with the coarse focusing knob while you are looking down the microscope?

i) If the magnifying power of the eyepiece lens is ten times (×10), and that of the low power objective lens is four times (×4), what is the total magnification of a specimen under low power?

Topic 4 Investigating cells

j) If the magnifying power of the eyepiece lens is ×10, and that of the high power objective lens is ×40, what is the total magnification of a specimen under high power?

2 Copy this diagram of a **typical animal cell** and label the cell membrane, cytoplasm and nucleus.

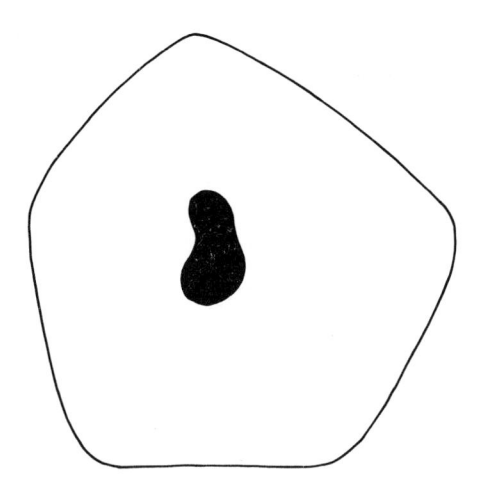

3 Copy this diagram of a **typical plant cell** and label the following:

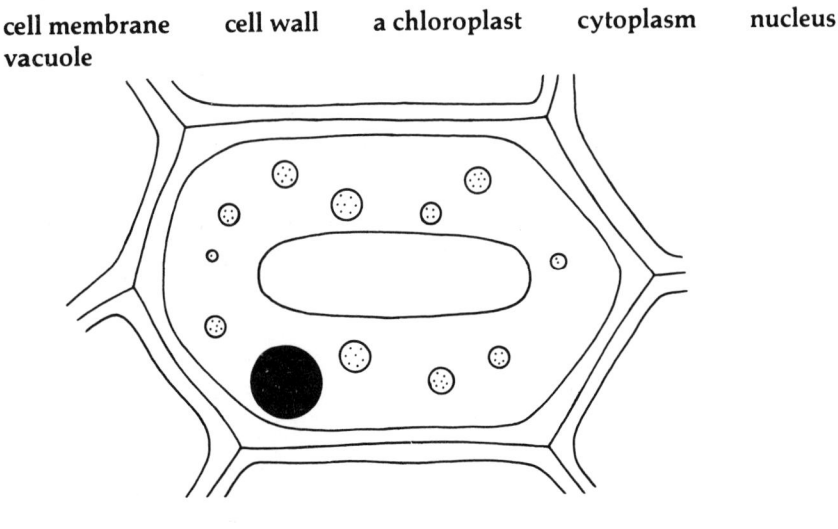

cell membrane   **cell wall**   **a chloroplast**   **cytoplasm**   **nucleus**
vacuole

Did You Know?
In an average lifetime we shed about 20 kilograms of dead skin cells.

4 Copy the table below. Complete it by putting a tick if the structure in the first column is present and a cross if it is not.

Structure	Typical animal cell (e.g. cheek cell)	Typical plant cell (e.g. moss leaf cell)
Cell membrane		
Cell wall		
Chloroplasts		
Cytoplasm		
Nucleus		
Vacuole		

Did You Know?
A fully grown human is made up of about one hundred million million cells.

5 Match the following cell structures with their correct description:

Cell Structure	Description
cell membrane	the granular material in which the nucleus is embedded
cell wall	a large fluid-filled cavity in the middle of a plant cell
chloroplasts	thread-like bodies found inside the nucleus
chromosomes	a thin structure which surrounds the cytoplasm
cytoplasm	the structure which controls the cytoplasm; without it, the cell almost always dies
nucleus	structures which contain the green pigment chlorophyll
vacuole	the outer boundary of plant cells; made of cellulose

6 Below are five pairs of statements about animal or plant cells. Sort them into two groups:

Animal cells	Plant cells

a) They are surrounded only by a thin cell membrane.
   They have a cellulose cell wall in addition to a cell membrane.

b) They have a large central vacuole.
   They do not have a large central vacuole.

Topic 4 Investigating cells

c) The cytoplasm fills the cell.
   The cytoplasm is pushed towards the edge of the cell.

d) The cytoplasm contains chloroplasts.
   The cytoplasm does not contain chloroplasts.

e) Food is stored as starch.
   Food is stored as glycogen.

7 a) Place these **units of length** in order starting with the smallest unit and ending with the largest:

   kilometre   metre   micrometre   millimetre   nanometre

b) **Bacteria** are microscopic organisms. They cannot be seen with the naked eye. The best units of length for measuring bacteria are micrometres.

   1000 micrometres = 1 millimetre

   i) A typical bacterium is about a thousandth of a millimetre wide. How many micrometres is this?

   ii) How many micrometres are there in one metre?

   iii) Millimetres can be written as mm. How can we write micrometres for short?

2 Diffusion and Osmosis

1 Copy and complete this sentence, choosing the correct word given in the brackets:

   Diffusion results in molecules moving from a region of (high/low) concentration to a region where they are (less/more) concentrated.

2 Copy and complete the following sentences (a–f) by filling in the missing words:

   a) **Diffusion** is important because it is the main way in which living organisms obtain the things they ___need___, and get rid of their ___waste___ products. Here are some examples.

   b) Oxygen continually ___diffused___ into the body of *Amoeba* and ___CO_2___ continually diffuses out. This is because *Amoeba* constantly uses ___O_2___ and produces ___CO_2___.

   c) The same process also occurs in our lungs. The ___O_2___ diffuses from the lungs into the blood. The ___CO_2___ diffuses from the blood into the lungs.

   d) In our gut soluble food substances such as glucose ___move___ from the intestine into the surrounding blood capillaries.

Topic 4 Investigating cells

e) Green leaves obtain the gas __CO_2__ for photosynthesis by diffusion. It enters the leaf through small holes or pores.

f) Fishes obtain __O_2__ from the water by diffusion. As the water flows past the gills, oxygen __diffuses__ from the water into the blood. Carbon dioxide diffuses from the __blood__ into the water.

3 Copy and complete this sentence about **osmosis** by filling in the missing words:

Osmosis involves the movement of __water__ through a __selectively permeable__ membrane.

4 Consider the diagram below. Some of the following statements about it are true, and others are false. Decide which are the correct statements and write them down.

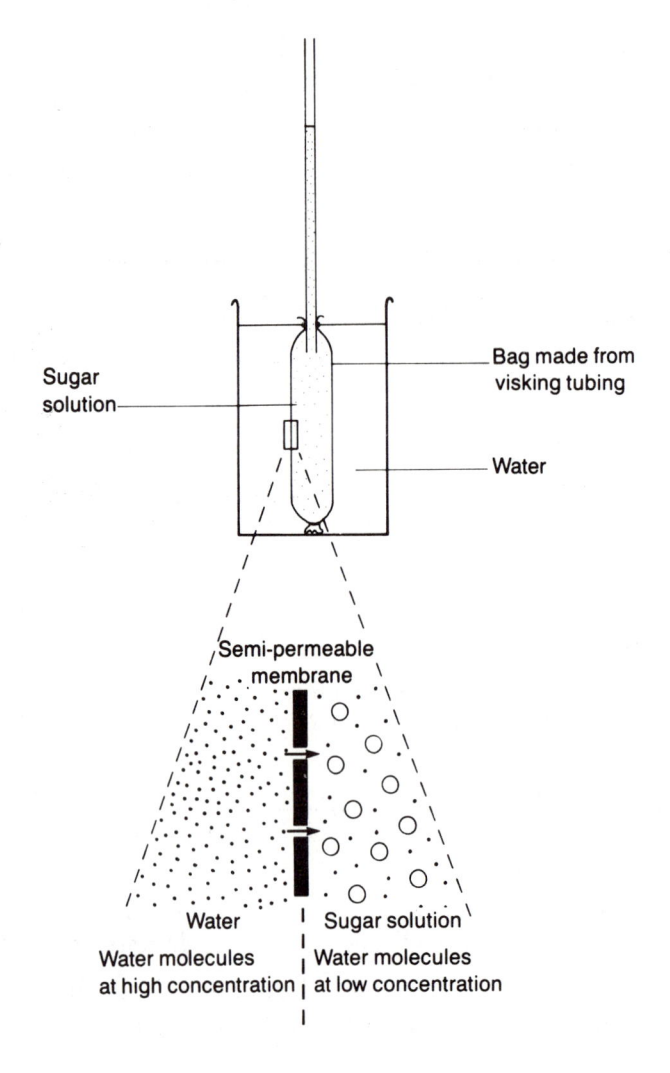

Topic 4 Investigating cells

a) All the molecules are the same size.
b) Water molecules are smaller than sugar molecules. ✓
c) Water molecules can pass in and out of the bag. ✓
d) Sugar molecules can pass in and out of the bag.
e) Sugar molecules cannot pass out of the bag. ✓
f) There are more water molecules inside the bag.
g) There are more water molecules outside the bag. ✓
h) Water molecules move from low to high concentration.
i) Water molecules move from high to low concentration. ✓
j) Water molecules move into the bag. ✓
k) Water molecules move out of the bag.
l) Sugar molecules move out of the bag.
m) Sugar molecules move into the bag.
n) The volume of the bag increases. ✓
o) The volume of the bag decreases.
p) The level of the liquid in the tube rises. ✓
q) The level of the liquid in the tube falls.
r) The water level in the beaker rises.
s) The water level in the beaker falls. ✓

5 Suppose a semi-permeable bag (as in question 4) was filled with a 20% sugar solution. What would happen to the volume of liquid inside the bag if it was surrounded by the following? Give reasons in each case.

a) distilled water — increase
b) 5% sugar solution — ″
c) 20% sugar solution — same
d) 40% sugar solution — decrease

6 Copy and complete the following sentences (a–d) about animal cells and osmosis. Choose the best word or words from the three alternatives given.

a) Animal cells contain ...
   i) salt.
   ii) a solution of salts and other substances. ✓
   iii) water.

b) Animal cells are enclosed by ...
   i) a cell wall.
   ii) a permeable membrane.
   iii) a selectively permeable membrane. ✓

c) When placed in water animal cells ...
   i) swell up and burst. ✓
   ii) shrink and wrinkle.
   iii) remain the same.

d) When animal cells are put into a strong salt solution they ...
   i) swell up and burst.
   ii) shrink and wrinkle. ✓
   iii) remain the same.

7 a) Copy the diagram below and add the following labels:

   cell wall   cytoplasm   vacuole   root hair   soil particle
   soil water   nucleus

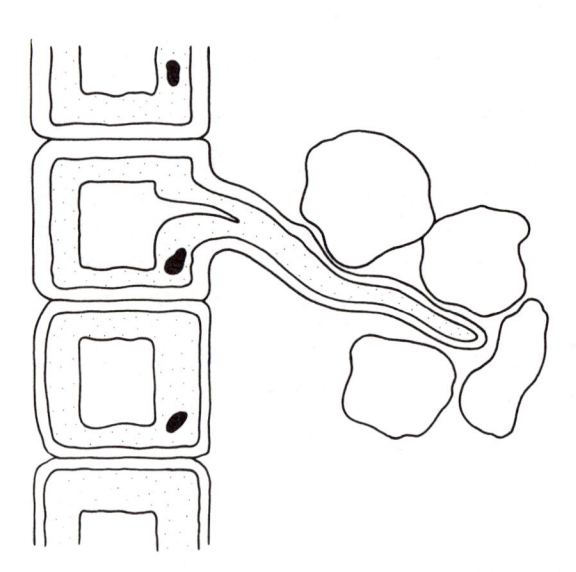

The diagram above represents part of a root in soil highly magnified.

b) How does water move from the soil into the root?

c) How do mineral salts enter the root cells?

Topic 4 Investigating cells

8 Copy and complete the following sentences about plant cells and osmosis. Choose the best answer from the three given.

a) In the centre of a plant cell there is a vacuole which contains ...
   i) salt.
   ii) a solution of salts and other substances.
   iii) water.

b) Plant cells are enclosed by ...
   i) a cell wall.
   ii) a cell membrane.
   iii) a cell wall and cell membrane.

c) The cell wall is ...
   i) fully permeable.
   ii) semi-permeable.
   iii) non-permeable.

d) The cell membrane is ...
   i) fully permeable.
   ii) semi-permeable.
   iii) non-permeable.

e) A plant cell put into water ...
   i) shrinks and crinkles.
   ii) swells and becomes turgid or firm.
   iii) remains the same.

f) A plant cell put into a strong salt solution ...
   i) swells and becomes turgid.
   ii) remains the same.
   iii) becomes soft and plasmolysed.

9 Below are two simple diagrams of plant cells in different conditions. Draw the cells and then answer the questions which follow.

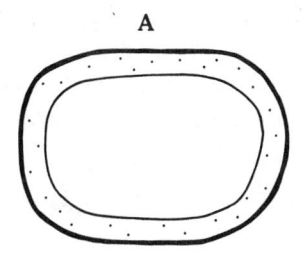

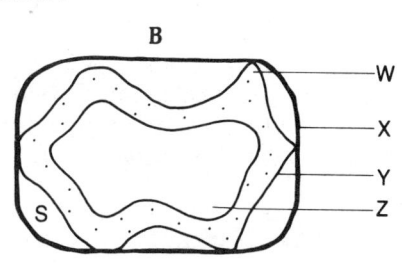

a) Which cell has been placed in distilled water?
b) Which cell has been placed in strong sugar solution?
c) Which cell is turgid?
d) Which cell is plasmolysed?
e) In plant cell B
   i) what do the labels W, X, Y and Z represent?
   ii) what is found in the space marked S?

10 a) Water constantly enters the body of freshwater *Amoeba* by osmosis. Explain why this happens.
b) What would happen to the *Amoeba* if it did not get rid of this water?
c) What is the function of the contractile vacuole in *Amoeba*?

The table following shows the results of an experiment with *Amoeba* in which it forms a contractile vacuole. An individual *Amoeba* was placed in different concentrations of salt solution. The average number of times the contractile vacuole formed and emptied in ten minutes was recorded.

Concentration of salt solution	Average number of times contractile vacuole forms and empties in ten minutes
0.5%	10
1.0%	8
1.5%	6
2.0%	4.5
2.5%	3
3.0%	2
5.0%	0

d) Plot a graph of these results. Put percentage salt solution on the horizontal axis.
e) In 5% salt solution the *Amoeba* was still moving, but no contractile vacuole was formed. Explain the reason for this.

3 Cell Division

1 When organisms grow they increase the number of cells they are made of. A single cell divides to form two cells. The two new cells must have chromosomes that are identical to those of the original cell from which they were formed. In this way all the cells of an organism will have a set of chromosomes identical to that of the single fertilised egg from which they grew.

a) What name is given to the type of cell division that produces two cells that are identical to the parent cell?

Topic 4 Investigating cells

b) Copy and complete the diagram below by drawing in the nuclei of the two cells produced when the original cell divides by **mitosis**.

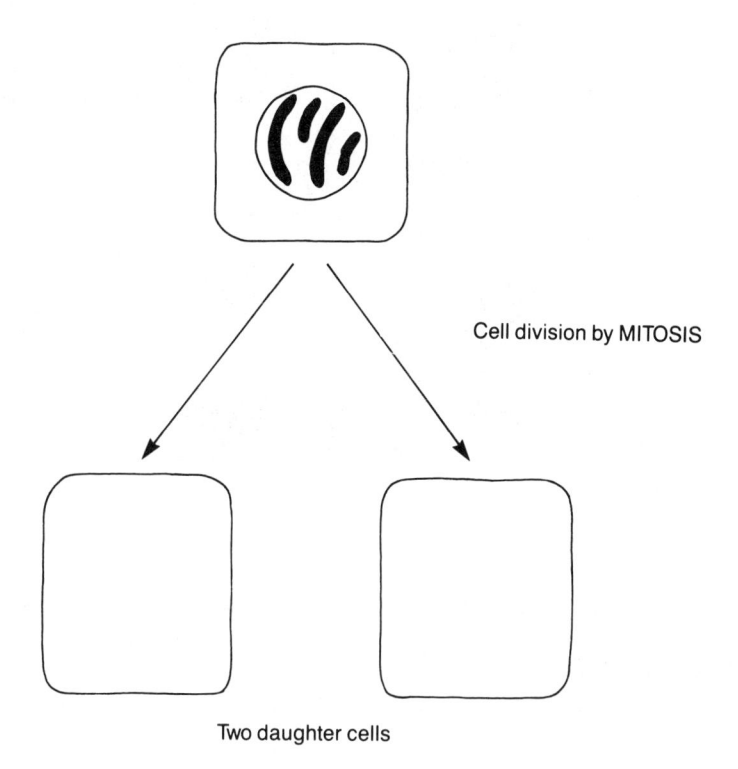

Cell division by MITOSIS

Two daughter cells

A cell of an imaginary organism with four chromosomes

2 a) When would mitosis occur in *Amoeba*?
   b) Where would you expect mitosis to occur in
      i) a growing plant, such as a tree in spring?
      ii) an adult human?
   c) Complete this sentence:
      Cells divide by mitosis during _____ and _____ reproduction.

3 The diagrams on the following page show stages in mitosis.
   a) Using the identifying letters arrange these stages in the correct sequence.
   b) Explain what is happening in each stage.

Topic 4 Investigating cells

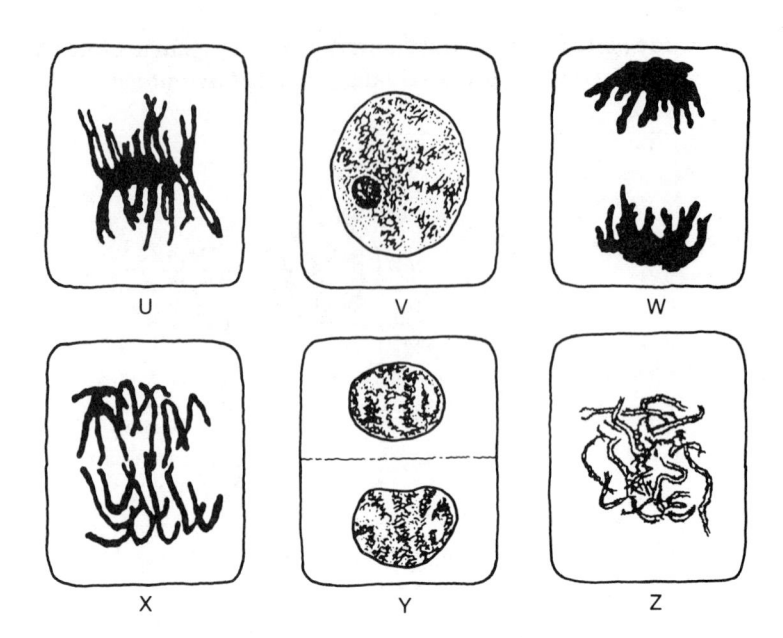

U V W

X Y Z

4 Enzymes

1 Choose words from this list to complete the following sentences about enzymes.

    catalysts   destroyed   neutral   organisms   control
    proteins   reactions   specific   catalyse

a) Enzymes are _____ which speed up or _____ the chemical _____ which occur in _____. They are 'biological _____ '.

b) Enzymes are _____ in that they can only control one type of reaction.

c) Enzymes are _____ by excess heat and are also sensitive to changes in pH. Most enzymes work best in _____ conditions.

d) Enzymes are important because they _____ where and when the cell's reactions take place.

2 Explain how you would test a solution for the presence of

a) starch

b) sugar

In each case, describe the result of a positive test.

Topic 4 Investigating cells

3 The following results were obtained from an experiment in which a solution of the enzyme amylase was mixed with a starch suspension. Samples of the mixture were kept in water baths at different temperatures for 15 minutes. At the end of this time the samples were analysed to find out how much sugar had been produced in each. The results are given below.

Temperature /°C	0	10	20	30	40	50	60	70	80
Units of sugar	12	36	65	90	90	60	30	4	2

a) Plot a line graph of these results, labelling the axes as shown.

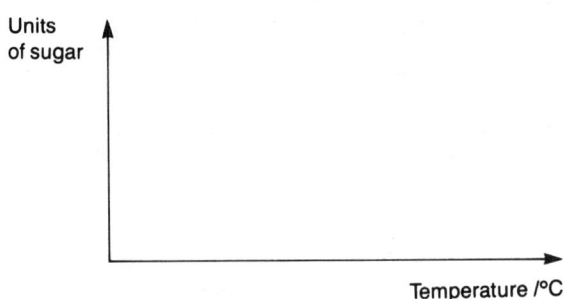

b) What is the action of amylase on starch?

c) At which temperature is most sugar produced?

d) Why is very little sugar formed when the amylase and starch mixture is kept at a high temperature?

e) What other factors, besides temperature, would affect the amount of sugar produced from a starch and amylase mixture?

f) Can amylase break down any substances other than starch? Explain your answer.

4 Hydrogen peroxide can be broken down by catalysts into water and oxygen. In an experiment to investigate this reaction, samples of fresh and previously boiled materials were added to samples of hydrogen peroxide in test-tubes. Any gas evolved was tested for oxygen. The results are shown on the next page.

a) What would you see happening in the test-tubes as gas is evolved.

b) How would you test the gas for oxygen?

c) Why was tube 1 set up?

d) Explain carefully what has happened in tube 2.

e) Explain the results which occur in tubes 4 and 6.

f) Explain why the result obtained in tube 3 differs from that in tubes 5 and 7.

g) State *two* factors which should be kept constant in all seven tubes.

Topic 4 Investigating cells

Test-tube	Contents	Test on gas evolved
1	Hydrogen peroxide	No oxygen evolved
2	Hydrogen peroxide + fresh manganese dioxide	Oxygen evolved
3	Hydrogen peroxide + boiled manganese dioxide	Oxygen evolved
4	Hydrogen peroxide + fresh liver	Oxygen evolved
5	Hydrogen peroxide + boiled liver	No oxygen evolved
6	Hydrogen peroxide + fresh blood	Oxygen evolved
7	Hydrogen peroxide + boiled blood	No oxygen evolved

5 Design an experiment to investigate the effect of a range of pH on the activity of catalase in liver. Sketch a graph of the results you would expect from such an experiment.

6 The table below shows the time taken for the complete breakdown of a sample of starch suspension in the presence of an enzyme in solutions of different pH.

Time taken/minutes	6	4.5	3	2	1.25	1.25	3
pH	5	5.5	6	6.5	7	7.5	8

a) Plot these results on graph paper, labelling the axes as shown:

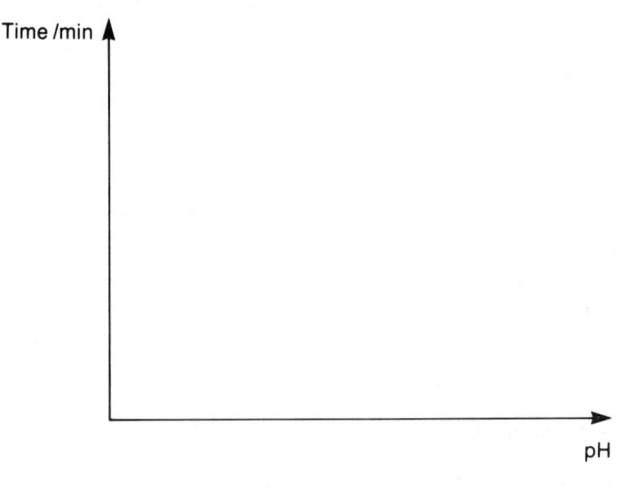

Time /min ▲

pH ▶

b) At what pH is there the fastest breakdown of the starch solution?

c) How would you prevent a change in temperature from affecting the results of this experiment?

d) Name one region of the gut where this enzyme would *not* work very quickly.

Topic 4 Investigating cells

e) Name one enzyme found in the region you have named.

f) Sketch a graph to show the effect of pH on the action of the enzyme you named in part e). (Put 'Rate of reaction' on the vertical axis.)

7 Explain the terms 'optimum temperature' and 'optimum pH' as applied to enzyme-controlled reactions.

5 Respiration

1 a) State three reasons why cells need **energy**.

b) What energy transformations occur

i) inside a chloroplast during photosynthesis?

ii) when a music cell contracts?

2 a) Copy and complete the following sentence about how energy is released. Choose the correct word or words from inside the brackets.

When a piece of food is burned, the gas (oxygen/carbon dioxide) is used up and (carbon dioxide/oxygen) is given off. Water is formed and heat energy is released.

b) Complete the following equation:

Food + ... ⟶ .... + water + energy

3 Which of the following descriptions are true of **respiration**?

a) occurs only in plant cells

b) occurs in all cells

c) takes place only at night

d) produces carbon dioxide

e) uses up energy

f) is affected by temperature

g) takes place all the time

h) produces food

i) produces oxygen

j) uses oxygen
k) uses carbon dioxide
l) produces water
m) releases energy
n) uses water
o) is controlled by enzymes

4 In what ways is respiration
  a) similar to, and
  b) different from, the **burning** of food?

5 When a peanut is burnt under a test-tube of water, as shown in the diagram, the water heats up.

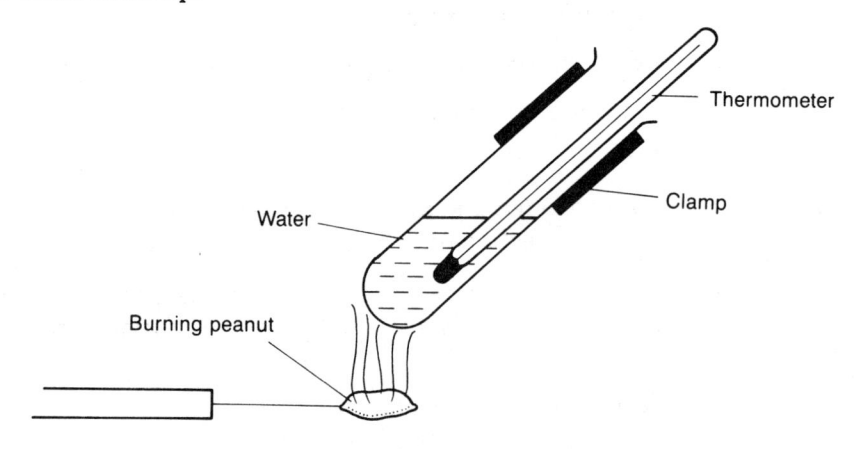

  a) What property of the peanut is being measured?
  b) What measurements must be taken before the peanut is set alight?
  c) State *two* safety precautions which must be taken when carrying out the experiment.
  d) What measurement must be taken after the peanut has finished burning?
  e) State *two* ways in which the result of the experiment may be inaccurate.
  f) What piece of apparatus could be used to produce a more accurate result?

6 The apparatus shown on the next page is used to measure the rate of respiration in germinating seeds.
  a) What is the purpose of the concentrated potassium hydroxide solution?
  b) What will happen to the coloured liquid in the capillary tubing as the seeds respire? Explain why this happens.

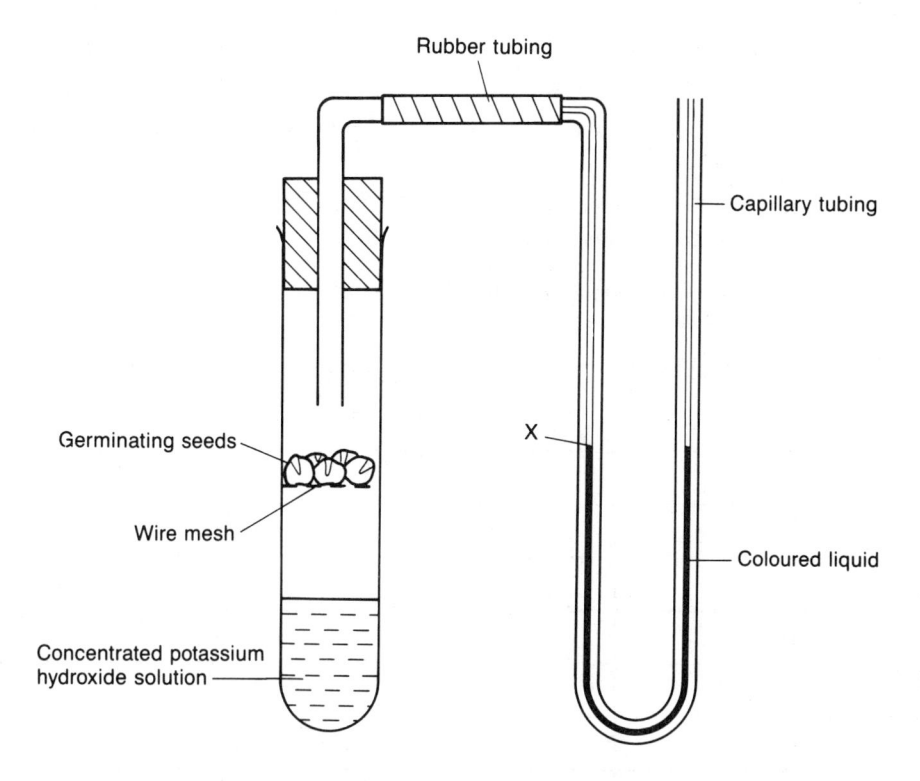

Topic 4 Investigating cells 99

[Diagram: Apparatus with test tube containing germinating seeds on wire mesh above concentrated potassium hydroxide solution, connected via rubber tubing to capillary tubing containing coloured liquid with level marked X.]

c) What control should be set up for this experiment?

d) Name two environmental factors that might affect the level of the liquid at X.

7 The experiment illustrated below was carried out to find out if living organisms give out heat energy.

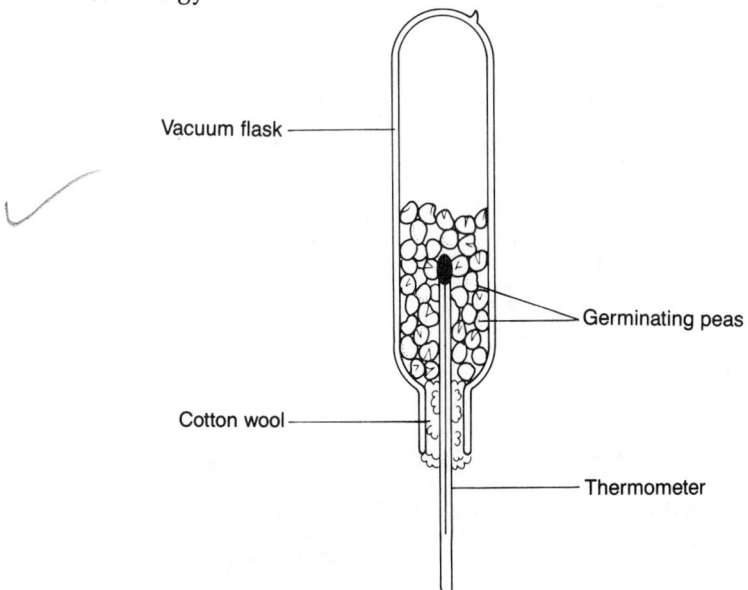

[Diagram: Vacuum flask containing germinating peas with thermometer inserted, sealed with cotton wool.]

Some pea seeds were divided into three samples of equal mass and then treated as follows:

Sample 1 was soaked in water at 18 °C for 24 hours, and then placed in a sterilised vacuum flask A.

Sample 2 was soaked in water at 18 °C for 24 hours, boiled, cooled to 18 °C and then placed in a sterilised vacuum flask B.

Sample 3 was soaked in water at 18 °C for 24 hours, washed with a very mild disinfectant, and then placed in a sterilised vacuum flask C.

The temperatures inside the three flasks were recorded for 3 days. They are shown below.

	Flask A	Flask B	Flask C
Start of experiment	18 °C	18 °C	18 °C
After 12 hours	26 °C	18 °C	20 °C
After 24 hours	40 °C	18 °C	23 °C
After 36 hours	48 °C	18 °C	26 °C
After 48 hours	50 °C	18 °C	29 °C
After 60 hours	52 °C	18 °C	33 °C
After 72 hours	54 °C	18 °C	40 °C

a) Plot the results for Flasks A, B and C on the same graph. Label the axes as shown.

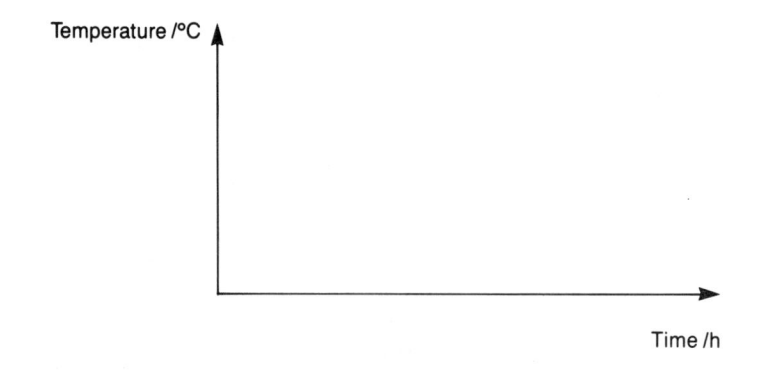

b) Why were vacuum flasks used instead of ordinary glass flasks?

c) What process caused the rise in temperature in Flasks A and C?

d) Why were the peas soaked before being placed in the flasks?

e) Why was there no temperature rise in Flask B?

Topic 4 Investigating cells

f) Why was the temperature rise greater in Flask A than Flask C?

g) Why was Flask B included in the experiment?

8 a) Listed below are seven pairs of descriptions of respiration and photosynthesis. Draw up a table and sort them into two groups:

Respiration	Photosynthesis

  i) occurs in all cells/occurs in green plant cells

 ii) energy is released/energy is stored

iii) produces carbon dioxide/produces oxygen

 iv) produces food/produces water

  v) uses oxygen/uses carbon dioxide

 vi) uses water/uses food

vii) occurs only in the light/occurs all the time

b) The air around us contains oxygen and carbon dioxide in amounts that do not vary very much. Using the information from the correctly completed table, explain why this is so.

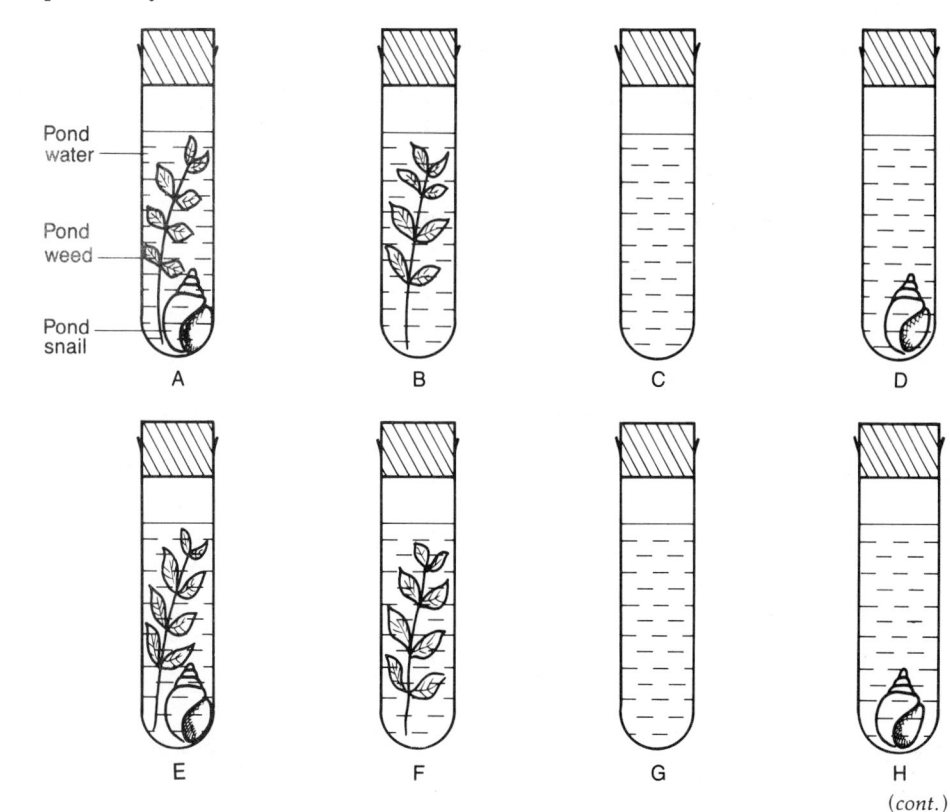

9

(cont.)

In an experiment, tubes A–H were set up as shown on the previous page. Tubes A–D were kept in bright light for several hours. Tubes E–H were kept in the dark for the same length of time. Red bicarbonate indicator was then added to each test-tube.

Bicarbonate indicator is used to show changes in carbon dioxide levels, which bring about a change in colour of the indicator.

Purple ←—— CO_2 levels decrease —— Red —— CO_2 levels increase ——→ Yellow

Bicarbonate indicator

a) Construct a table like the one below completing the results for each tube.

Tube	Respiration taking place?	Photosynthesis taking place?	CO_2 level unchanged, increased, or decreased?	Colour of indicator
C	X	X	Unchanged	Red

b) What effect does respiration have on carbon dioxide levels?

c) What effect does photosynthesis have on carbon dioxide levels?

d) Why were tubes C and G included?

e) Why were some tubes kept in the light and others in the dark?

f) In the light, photosynthesis proceeds at a faster rate than respiration. Which tubes show this? Explain your answer.

g) Why is the level of carbon dioxide in the atmosphere rising?

h) What is meant by the **greenhouse effect**, and why are scientists concerned about it?

Topic 5

The body in action

1 Movement

1 Below are some sentences to do with the **skeleton**. The middle part of each sentence has been missed out. Choose from the list below the best word or words to complete each sentence. Some may be used more than once. (The first one has been done for you as an example.)

> contains   protects   are made   is made of   makes
> connect   help in   works with   is protected by

The body ... is protected by ... the skeleton.

a) The skeleton _____ the soft organs of the body.
b) Blood cells _____ inside some bones.
c) The skeleton _____ muscles to bring about movement.
d) The skeleton _____ bone.
e) Bone _____ calcium.
f) Calcium _____ bones hard.
g) Tendons _____ muscles to bones.
h) Ligaments _____ bones to bones.
i) The skull _____ the brain.
j) The ribs _____ breathing.
k) The rib cage _____ the heart and lungs.
l) A moving joint _____ lubricating fluid.

2 Copy and complete this table about **joints**.

Joint	Type of joint: hinge or ball and socket
Hip	
Shoulder	
Elbow	
Knee	
Jaw	

Topic 5 The body in action

> *Did You Know?*
> Each of your hands has 27 bones, your spine has 26 and your skull 21.

3 Copy the diagram below, which represents a moving joint.

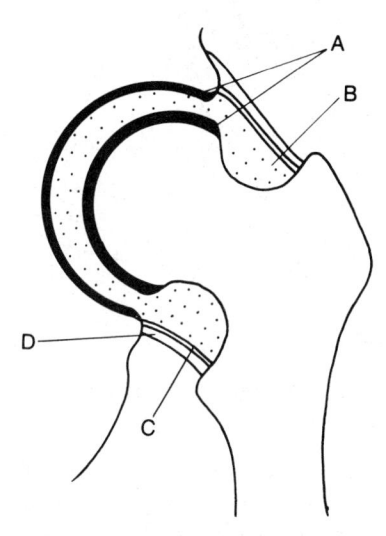

a) Replace the letters A to D with the correct labels.

b) Next to your diagram copy and complete this table:

	Name of structure	Function
A		
B		
C		
D		

> *Did You Know?*
> There are over 100 joints in your body and about 650 different muscles.

4 Study this diagram of the arm:

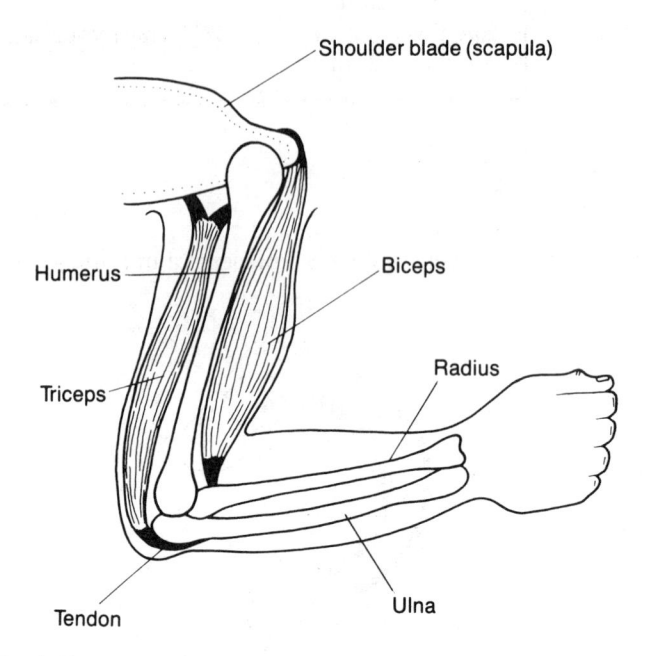

Complete the following passage by choosing the correct word or words from inside the brackets.

When you bend your arm at the elbow the following things happen:
The biceps (contracts/relaxes), becoming (shorter and fatter/longer and thinner). The triceps muscle (contracts/relaxes), becoming (shorter and fatter/longer and thinner). When you straighten your arm the (same/opposite) happens. The (triceps/biceps) muscle will do work when a weight is lifted off the ground.

2 The Need for Energy

1 a) Which of these substances provide the body with **energy**?

        carbohydrate   water   fat   mineral salts   protein   vitamins

  b) List *five* foods that provide lots of energy.

  c) List *five* foods that provide very little energy.

  d) What units are used to measure the energy value of food?

  e) Describe a simple experiment to show how much energy there is in a small piece of food such as a peanut.

Topic 5 The body in action

  f) Why does a coal-miner require more energy foods in his diet than a typist?
  g) Name one other occupation with a high daily energy need.
  h) Why does a woman's daily energy need increase when she is
    i) pregnant?
    ii) breast-feeding her baby?
  i) What happens if people consume more than their daily energy need?
  j) What happens if people consume less than their daily energy need?

> *Did You Know?*
> During an average lifetime a person eats 20–30 tonnes of food.

2 a) A healthy 15-year-old needs about 12 000 kilojoules a day. Using the tables below and on the next page, work out a well-balanced diet that meets these requirements.

  b) Make a list of all the food you have eaten in the last 24 hours. Using the tables calculate your daily energy intake.

Food	Energy value /kJ per portion
Fruit	
Dates	2140
Prunes	840
Banana	460
Pineapple	440
Cherries	390
Apple	380
Grapes	380
Pear	380
Grapefruit	300
Orange	300
Blackcurrants	250
Strawberries	240
Peach	170
Melon	120

Food	Energy value /kJ per portion
Meat	
Steak	2300
Lamb chop	1800
Beefburgers	1700
Sausages	1600
Roast lamb	1320
Bacon	1300
Roast beef	1100
Boiled ham	1000
Roast chicken	950
Luncheon meat	900
Liver	500
Kidney	300

(cont.)

Food	Energy value /kJ per portion
Vegetables	
Boiled rice	2600
Chips	1180
Boiled potatoes	500
Baked beans	500
Sweetcorn	350
Peas	230
Brussels sprouts	180
Tomatoes	120
Cabbage	80
Carrots	80
Cauliflower	80
Celery	80
Onions	80
Spinach	80
Lettuce	40
Runner beans	40
Fish	
Fried cod	800
Kipper	800
Sardines	800
Grilled cod	680
Tinned salmon	500
Cereals	
Porridge	630
Cornflakes	380
Puffed wheat	200

Food	Energy value /kJ per portion
Dairy Produce	
Milk (250 ml)	500
Cheddar cheese	460
Butter	420
Margarine	420
Boiled eggs	380
Whipped cream	210
Cottage cheese	100
Preserves	
Honey	680
Syrup	670
Jam	640
Marmalade	640
Sweets	
Chocolate (60 g)	1380
Toffee (60 g)	1060
Boiled sweets (60 g)	950
Other foods	
Peanuts (50 g)	1320
Spaghetti	690
Cakes	500
Ice-cream	460
Biscuits	450
Bread (slice)	270
Sugar (teaspoon)	100
Drinks	
Squash	450
Lemonade	420
Coffee with milk	110
Tea with milk	70

Topic 5 The body in action

3 Many experiments can be done to find out if organisms give out **carbon dioxide**. Here is one of them:

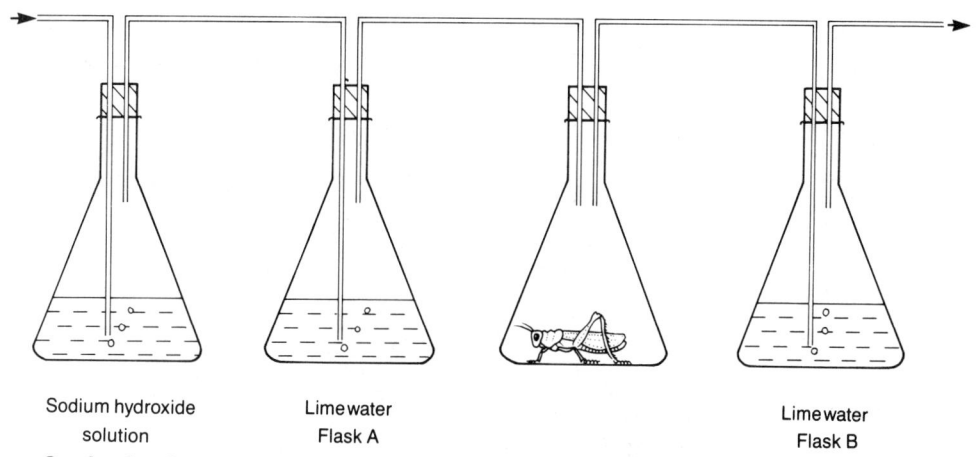

Sodium hydroxide solution

Limewater Flask A

Limewater Flask B

Study the diagram carefully and answer these questions:

a) What does the sodium hydroxide do?

b) What does the limewater in flask A show?

c) What change would you expect to take place in the limewater in flask B after 1 hour?

d) What control would you use in this investigation?

e) Why is it important to use a control?

4 Study the table below and then answer the questions.

	Air breathed in (inhaled air)	Air breathed out (exhaled air)
Nitrogen	79.0%	79.0%
Oxygen	20.97%	16.9%
Carbon dioxide	0.03%	4.1%
Water vapour	variable	saturated

a) What happens to the nitrogen we breathe in?

b) Which air sample contains the more oxygen? Explain why.

c) Which air sample contains the more carbon dioxide? Explain why.

d) What does 'saturated' mean?

e) Why does the amount of water vapour in the air vary?

5 a) Copy the diagram below, which represents the **human respiratory system**.

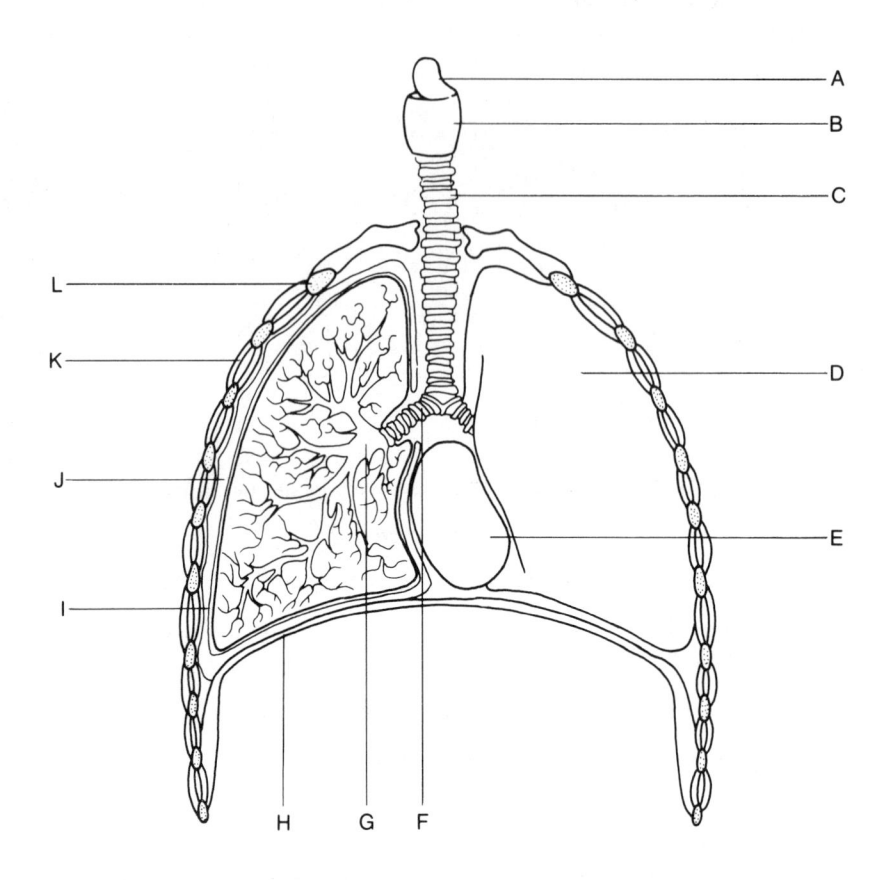

b) Replace the letters A to L with the correct label chosen from the list below:

bronchiole   bronchus   diaphragm   epiglottis   heart
larynx   lung   pleural fluid   pleural membranes   ribs
rib muscle   trachea

c) The diagram shows a vertical section through the human thorax. Why is the left lung smaller than the right?

6 From the two lists below, match each structure with its correct function. (The first one has been done for you as an example.)

The nasal cavity . . . warms, moistens and filters the air we breathe

Structure	Function
a) **The nasal cavity**	protect the lungs and heart
b) **The epiglottis**	separates the thorax from the abdomen
c) **The larynx**	move the rib cage during breathing

Topic 5 The body in action

	Structure	Function
d)	The trachea	that gas exchange takes place
e)	The cartilage rings	produces sounds
f)	The ribs	carries air down to the lungs
g)	The intercostal (or rib) muscles	help to keep the trachea and bronchi open
h)	The pleural fluid	prevents food from entering the trachea
i)	The diaphragm	warms, moistens and filters the air we breathe
j)	It is in the alveoli	prevents friction between the lungs and ribs when breathing

7 Below are eight pairs of statements about **breathing**. Sort them into two groups:

When we breathe in	When we breathe out

a) Intercostal muscles contract/Intercostal muscles relax.
b) The rib cage moves up and out/The rib cage moves down and in.
c) The diaphragm muscle relaxes/The diaphragm muscle contracts.
d) The diaphragm moves up/The diaphragm moves down.
e) The diaphragm becomes flatter/The diaphragm becomes dome-shaped.
f) The volume of thorax decreases/The volume of thorax increases.
g) The pressure inside the thorax decreases/The pressure inside the thorax increases.
h) Air is drawn into the lungs/Air is expelled from the lungs.

Did You Know?
You breathe about 20 000 litres of air every day.

8

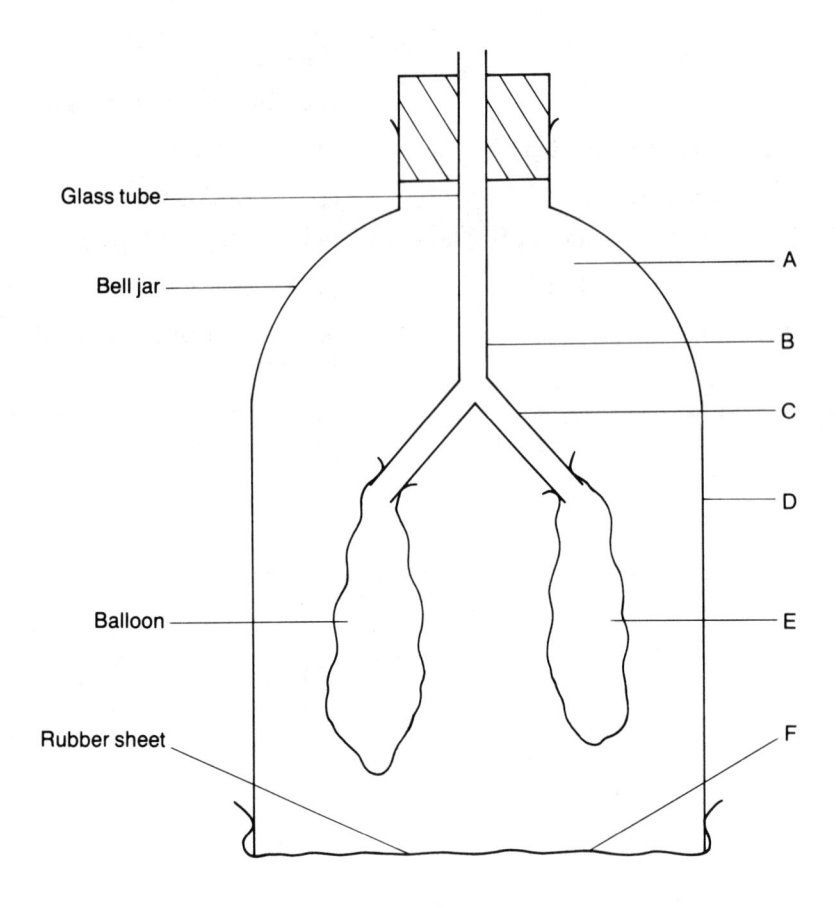

Labels on diagram: Glass tube, Bell jar, Balloon, Rubber sheet, A, B, C, D, E, F

The diagram above represents a model of the human **thorax**.

a) What parts of the human thorax do the labels A to F represent?

b) What happens to the balloons when the rubber sheet is pushed upwards? What part of breathing does this represent?

c) What happens to the balloons when the rubber sheet is pulled downwards? What part of breathing does this represent?

d) In what way is this an inaccurate demonstration of how we breathe in and out?

Did You Know?
There are about 300–750 million alveoli in your lungs.

Topic 5 The body in action

9 a) Make a large copy of the following diagram which shows how **gas exchange** occurs:

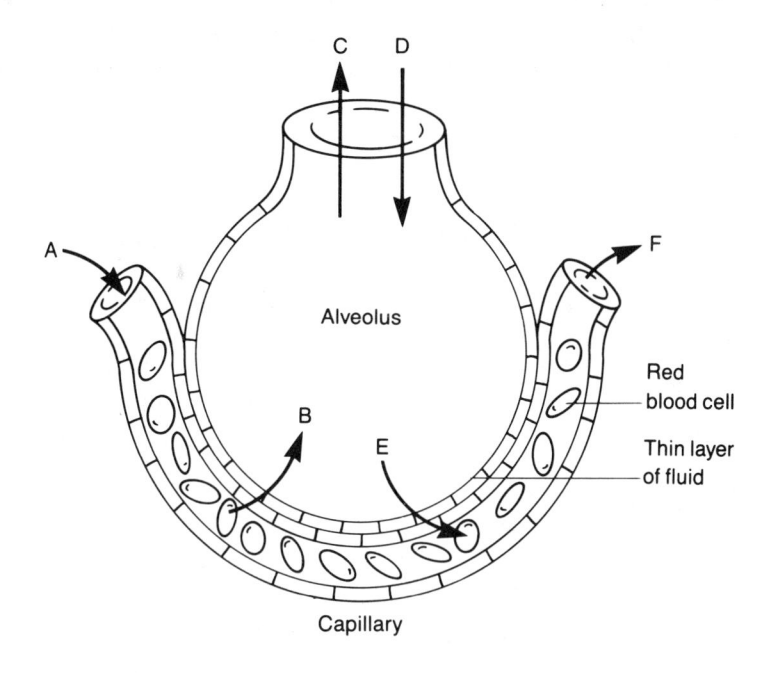

b) Explain what is happening at each of the stages labelled A–F.

10 Complete the following passage about **gas exchange** in the lungs by filling in the missing words:

Blood arrives at the lungs in the _____ arteries. This blood is deoxygenated. Oxygen has been used up by the cells of the body during the process of _____. This blood also contains a lot of _____. Each pulmonary artery branches many times to form very small vessels called _____. These are in direct contact with the tiny _____ of the lungs. It is here that _____ exchange takes place. _____ diffuses out of the blood. _____ diffuses into the blood. Oxygenated blood then leaves the lungs in the _____ vein.

11 Listed below are some features of the alveolar or respiratory surface of the lungs. Say why each feature makes the lung well suited to gas exchange.

Feature	Why it is well suited to gas exchange?
Thin	
Moist	
Large surface area	
Rich blood supply	

12 Here is a simple way to draw a ventral view of the **heart:**

a) Take a full clear page and in the middle draw *very lightly* in pencil, a box 12 cm high and 8 cm wide. Then divide the box into four, so that the top two boxes now measure 4 cm × 4 cm each, and the bottom two 8 cm × 4 cm each.

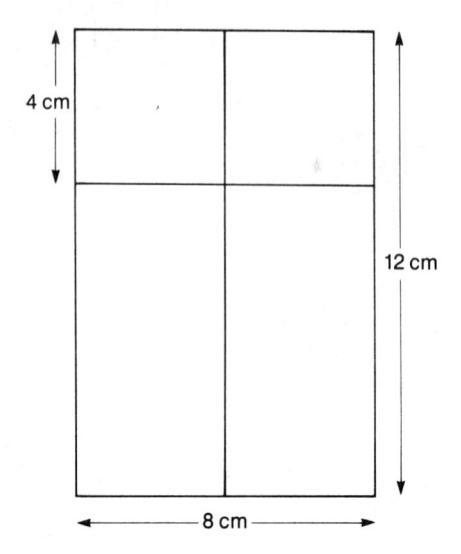

b) Sketch in lightly the shape of the heart and valve as shown below. (This is a ventral view, so the right side of the heart is on the left, and the left side is on the right.)

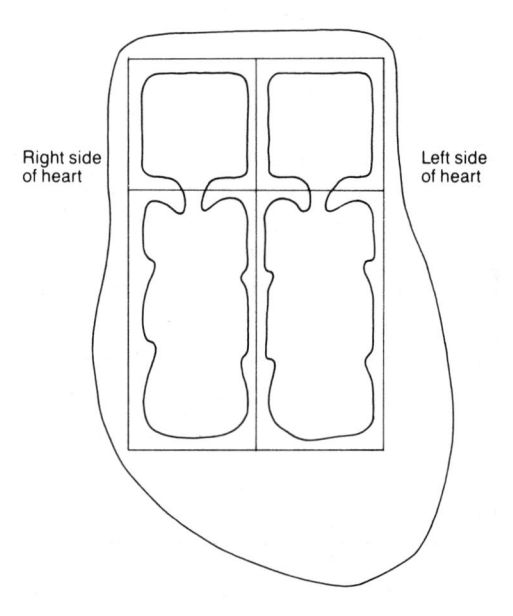

c) Carefully remove the box lines with a rubber.

d) Add the veins – like this:

Topic 5 The body in action

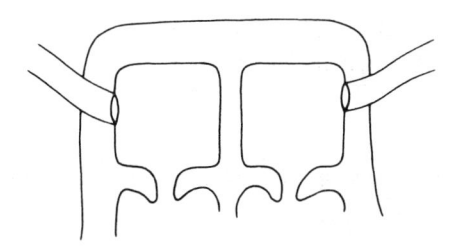

e) Finally add the arteries and their valves:

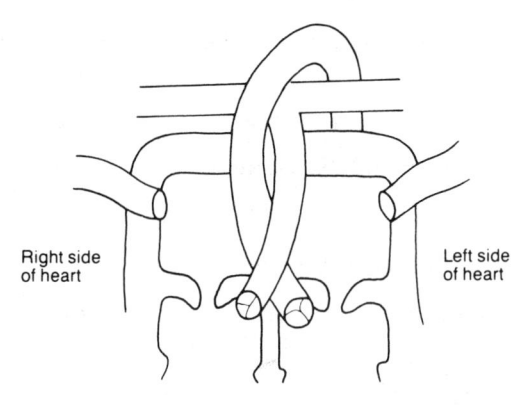

Right side of heart   Left side of heart

f) Now add the following labels to your diagram. Remember this is a *ventral* view.

right atrium   left atrium   right ventricle   left ventricle
vena cava   pulmonary artery   aorta   pulmonary vein
right atrioventricular valve   left atrioventricular valve
arterial (semi-lunar) valves

g) Now colour
   i) the heart muscle lightly in brown
   ii) the vena cava and pulmonary artery lightly in blue (explaining why)
   iii) the pulmonary vein and dorsal aorta lightly in red (explaining why)

13 On your diagram put small arrows to show the route the blood takes as it flows through the heart.

14 a) Put the following words in the correct sequence to show the order in which the blood flows through the heart. Start with the blood arriving at the heart from the body in the vena cava.

left ventricle   vena cava   opening between left atrium and ventricle
right atrium   aorta   opening between right atrium and ventricle
left atrium   right ventricle   pulmonary vein   pulmonary artery
lungs

b) Once you have done this correctly, describe in a few sentences the route that blood takes through the heart.

15 Answer the following questions about the heart:
a) What type of tissue is the heart made of?
b) What structures inside the heart keep the blood flowing in the right direction?
c) What is the function of the heart strings?
d) Explain why the walls of the ventricles are much thicker than those of the atria.
e) Which chamber of the heart has the thickest wall and why?
f) Why is the blood that passes through the right side of the heart deoxygenated?
g) Which chamber pumps blood to the lungs?
h) Which chamber is the first to receive oxygenated blood from the lungs?
i) Explain why the wall of the aorta is thicker than the wall of the pulmonary artery.
j) List *three* ways in which blood in the pulmonary artery differs from blood in the pulmonary vein.
k) There are many blood vessels running over the surface of the heart; what is their function?
l) Some babies are born with a 'hole in the heart', which means that there is a hole between the left and right atria. What problems does this cause?

16 Copy the plan of the **circulation** on the next page. Colour the arteries and the pulmonary vein red and the veins and the pulmonary artery blue.

Using the letters A to D mark on your diagram the blood vessel which has

A the highest pressure
B the most oxygen
C the most carbon dioxide
D the least urea

> *Did You Know?*
> The total length of arteries, veins and capillaries in your body is about 100 000 kilometres! The circumference of the earth is about 40 000 kilometres.

Topic 5 The body in action

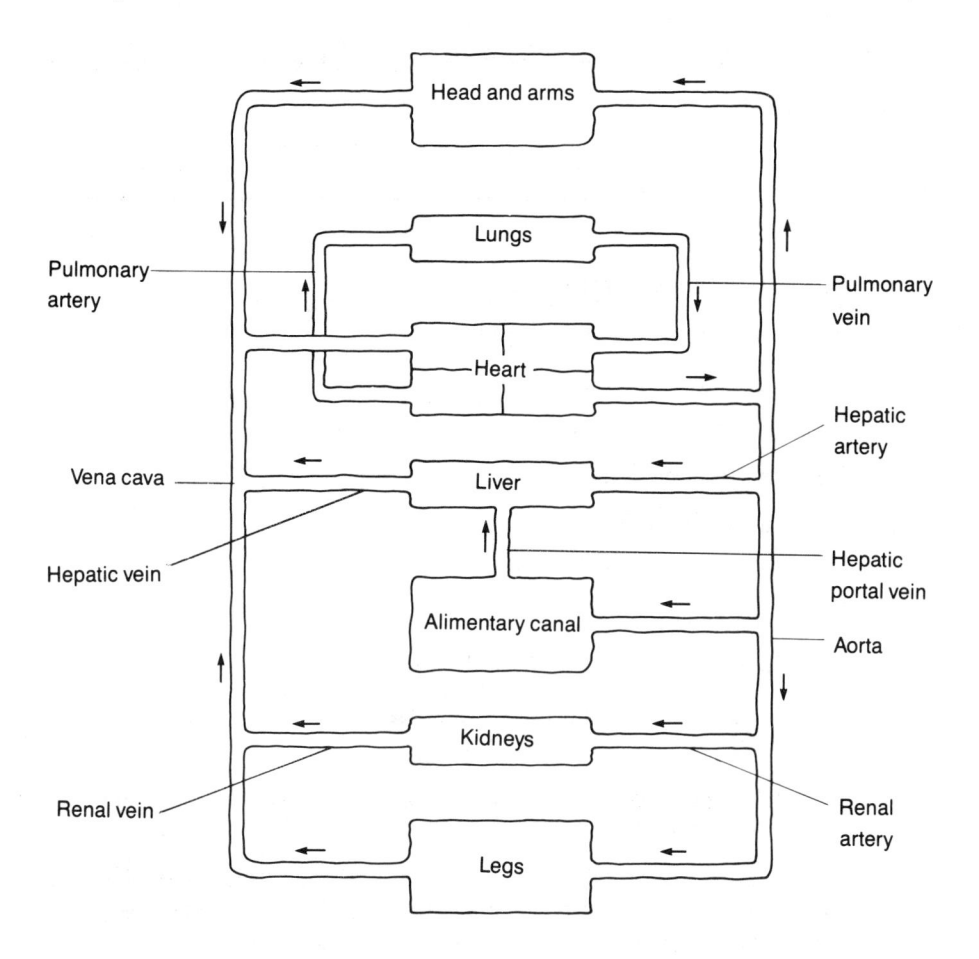

[Diagram of circulatory system with labels: Head and arms, Lungs, Heart, Liver, Alimentary canal, Kidneys, Legs, Pulmonary artery, Pulmonary vein, Vena cava, Hepatic artery, Hepatic vein, Hepatic portal vein, Aorta, Renal vein, Renal artery]

17 a) Use the words from this list to complete the following passage about **heart disease**. (If necessary you may use a word more than once).

  atheroma   beating   blocked   coronary   death   fatty
  heart attack   oxygen

The heart muscle receives blood from the _____ arteries. If one of these vessels becomes _____ the heart muscle in that area stops _____ because it is being starved of nutrients and _____. This is called a _____. It often occurs quite suddenly and is a very common cause of _____. Many factors contribute to heart disease, although the blockage itself is often caused by _____ material deposited in the _____ arteries. This is called an _____.

b) Below is a list of factors thought to be related to heart disease. For each one write one or two sentences which briefly explain how it contributes to the disease.

  diet   smoking   excess alcohol consumption
  lack of physical exercise   stress   obesity   high blood pressure
  inherited weakness   age

18 Listed below are some properties of types of **blood vessel**. Separate them into three groups as follows:

Arteries	Veins	Capillaries

a) carry blood to the heart
b) carry blood from the heart
c) have thick elastic walls
d) have walls one cell thick
e) carry blood under high pressure
f) carry blood under low pressure
g) have thin muscular walls
h) oxygen and food pass through the walls
i) have valves to prevent back-flow
j) blood flows through them in pulses

19 Complete the following passages about the carriage of oxygen by filling in the missing words:

_____ blood cells contain haemoglobin. When these cells pass through the lungs, the haemoglobin combines with _____ to form oxyhaemoglobin. In this way oxygen is carried around the body to the _____. Here the _____ is released and oxyhaemoglobin is turned back into _____.

20 If some blood is put into a small tube and spun at high speed in a centrifuge, the two main parts of the blood can be seen, i.e. the plasma (water and dissolved substances) and the blood cells (red and white).

a) 90 per cent of the plasma is water but what of the remainder? Make a list of all those things you would expect to find in the remaining ten per cent.

b) Make a list of as many functions of blood as you can.

21 If the average **heart rate** is 70 beats per minute how many times does the heart beat

a) in an hour?
b) in a day?
c) in a week?
d) in a year?
e) in 70 years?

3 Co-ordination

1 Match the words in the left-hand column with those in the right-hand column.

respiration	producing offspring
nutrition	movement from place to place
excretion	releasing energy from food
reproduction	responding to stimuli
sensitivity	feeding
locomotion	getting rid of poisonous waste

2 Name *five* stimuli to which human beings are sensitive.

3 Copy and complete this table about the **senses of the body**. Some of the gaps have already been filled in for you.

Name of sense receptor/organ	Where is it found in the body?	What is it sensitive to?
Touch receptor	skin	
Pain receptor		
		hot and cold
	tongue	
	on the front of the head	light
Ear		
	nose	
Semicircular canals		

Did You Know?
The skin contains about 4 million receptors sensitive to pain, temperature, pressure and touch.

4

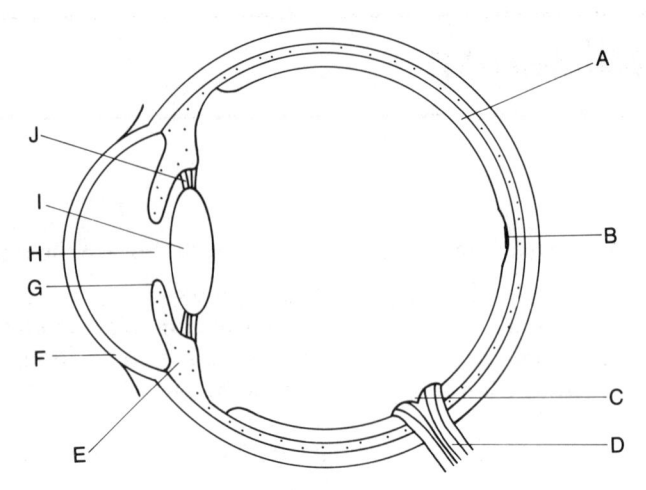

Make a large copy of the above diagram of **the eye** and replace the letters A to J with the correct label chosen from the following list:

    blind spot   ciliary muscle   cornea   iris   lens   ligaments
    optic nerve   upil   retina   yellow spot

> *Did You Know?*
> Your eyes are able to see nearly 8 million shades of colour.

5 Match the following words and phrases to make correct sentences about the eye and seeing. Each sentence should begin with one of the phrases on the left and finish with one on the right. The first one has been done for you as an example:

    The iris consists of . . . circular and radial muscles.

a) The iris consists of   shape.
b) The retina contains   impulses to the brain.
c) The yellow spot contains   circular and radial muscles.
d) The blind spot has   millions of light sensitive cells.
e) The ligaments hold   only cones.
f) The pupil allows   no light-sensitive cells.
g) The cornea bends the   the lens.
h) The lens can change   light to enter the eye.
i) The optic nerve carries   light rays.

> *Did You Know?*
> Your eyes have about 125 million rods and 7 million cones.

Topic 5 The body in action

6 Copy the passage below and fill in the gaps with words from the following list:

    radial   larger   smaller   circular   relax(es)   contract(s)
    less   retina

(Some words may be used more than once.)

In bright light the pupil becomes _____, owing to the action of the iris. The iris consists of _____ and _____ muscles. When one _____ the other _____. In bright light, the _____ muscles relax and the _____ muscles _____; thus the pupil becomes _____, allowing _____ light to fall on the _____ at the back of the eye.

> **Did You Know?**
> Your eye muscles move 100 000 times a day.

7 a) Copy this diagram of the **human ear**:

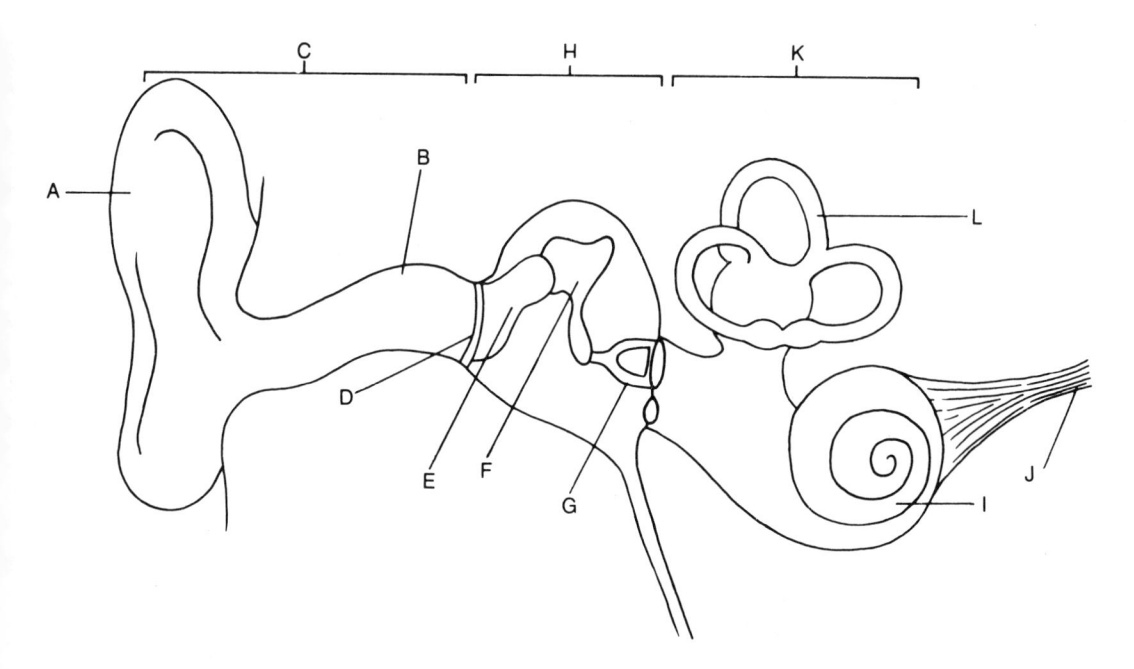

b) Replace the letters A to L with the correct label chosen from the list below.

    anvil   auditory nerve   cochlea   ear-drum
    external ear channel   hammer   inner ear   middle ear
    outer ear   pinna   semicircular canals   stirrup

Topic 5 The body in action

8 Consider the words following, which refer to either the eye or the ear (or both). Copy the headings below and then decide which word belongs under which heading:

The eye	The ear	Both

sound   focus   retina   deaf   light   frequency
blind   loud   hammer   cochlea pupil   auditory nerve
soft   anvil   blind spot iris   dim   cornea   ear-drum
cataracts wax   vibrate   lens   bright   stirrup   pressure
optic nerve

9 As sound passes through the ear, it comes into contact with the following structures:

hammer   cochlea   stirrup   anvil   outer ear canal
ear-drum auditory nerve   brain

Starting with the outer ear canal, place these structures in the correct order.

Did You Know?
There are more than 20 000 sensory hair cells in the cochlea.

10 Here are seven sentences about the ear and hearing. The middle part of each sentance has been missed out. Choose from the list below the best word or words to complete each sentence. Some may be used more than once. (The first one has been done for you as an example.)

Two ears ... help to ... tell us where sound comes from.

a) Two ears   _____ tell us where sound comes from.
b) The ear wax helps to _____ dust and germs from entering the ear.
c) The ear-drum   _____ the outer and middle ear chambers.
d) The three ear bones _____ the sound vibrations.
e) The cochlea   _____ fluid and sensory cells.
f) Sensory cells   _____ vibrations of the fluid.
g) Loud sounds can   _____ deafness.

help to   prevent   respond to   contains   cause
transmit and amplify   separates

Topic 5 The body in action

11 Complete this passage about how we hear:

Sound waves are directed into the external ear canal by the _____. The waves cause the _____ to vibrate. The vibrations are magnified many times as they pass along the three tiny ear ossicles in the _____ ear chamber. The ossicles are called the _____, _____ and _____. The membrane covering the oval window then vibrates and causes fluid in the cochlea to move. This stimulates tiny sensory hair _____. A nervous impulse is sent along the _____ nerve to the _____, which interprets the message and the sound is heard.

12 When we respond to stimuli, three things are needed:

a) Sense organs, e.g. eyes, ears, etc. (*Clue words:* stimuli, detect)

b) Nerves (*Clue word*: impulses)

c) Muscles or glands (*Clue words:* contract, move, bones, secrete)

Write down in sentences why each of these is important.

13 Copy and complete the following sentences, filling in the missing words:

When our receptors are stimulated _____ nerve cells relay the impulse to the central nervous system. Here the _____ is sorted out. Impulses are then relayed from the CNS to our muscles along _____ nerve cells.

14 We respond to stimuli all the time.

a) Make a list of at least *six* stimuli to which you have responded in one day. Here are two examples to help you:

Stimulus   *Response*
I hear the telephone ringing   I pick up the receiver
I feel cold   I put on a pullover

b) Now think of some responses given by organisms other than humans. Write down as many as you can.

c) Match the following groups of words to make correct sentences about the nervous system. Each sentence should begin with the words on the left and finish with the words on the right.

The job of the nervous system	sensory and motor nerve fibres.
The central nervous system (CNS)	is to carry nerve messages around the body.
Nerves connect the CNS	little electrical pulses.
Nerve messages are	is composed of the brain and spinal cord.
Nerves are made up of	to all parts of the body.

15 Look at this diagram about **reflex action**, and starting with number 1 match each of the numbers with one of the statements below. For example, 1 = pain receptors in the foot are stimulated.

a) Impulse enters the spinal cord.
b) Impulse is sent up the spinal cord to the brain.
c) Pain receptors in the foot are stimulated.
d) Impulse travels along sensory nerve cell.
e) Impulse is received and sorted out by brain.
f) Impulse travels along the motor nerve cell.
g) Foot is removed from the sharp stimulus.
h) Impulse leaves the spinal cord.
i) Muscles in leg and foot contract.

Did You Know?
Some nerve impulses can travel at about 240 kilometres per hour.

Topic 5 The body in action

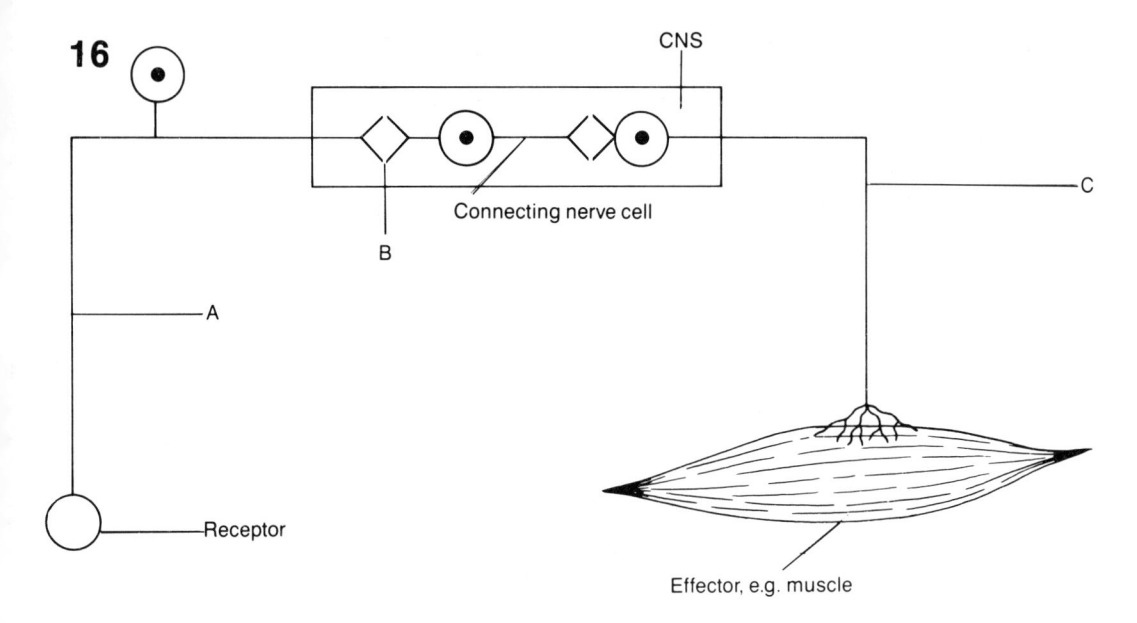

16

Receptor

Connecting nerve cell

CNS

Effector, e.g. muscle

Copy the diagram above. Replace the letters A to C with the correct label chosen from the list below.

sensory nerve cell   synapse   motor nerve cell

Also on the diagram, use arrows to show the direction in which the impulse travels.

17 a) Copy the following diagram of a reflex arc:

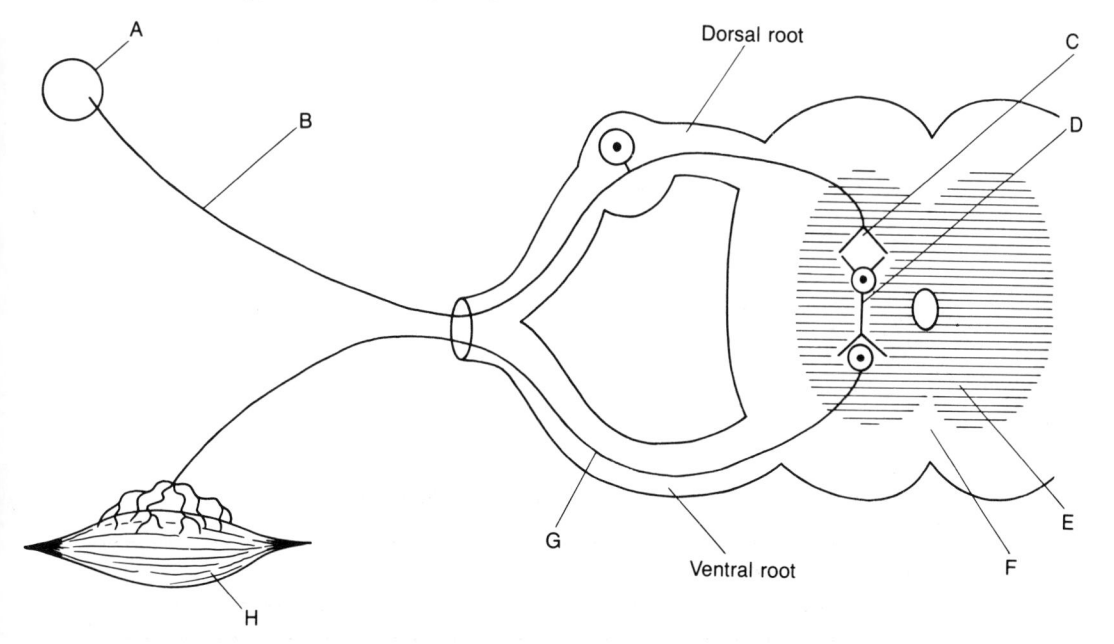

Dorsal root

Ventral root

b) Replace the letters A to H with the correct label chosen from the list below.

    grey matter in spinal cord   intermediate nerve fibre
    motor nerve fibre   muscle   receptor   sensory nerve fibre
    synapse   white matter in spinal cord

c) What would be the result if
   i) the dorsal root was cut?
   ii) the ventral root was cut?

Did You Know?
There are about 13 000 million nerve cells in your brain and nervous system.

18 a) Copy the following diagram of the **human brain**:

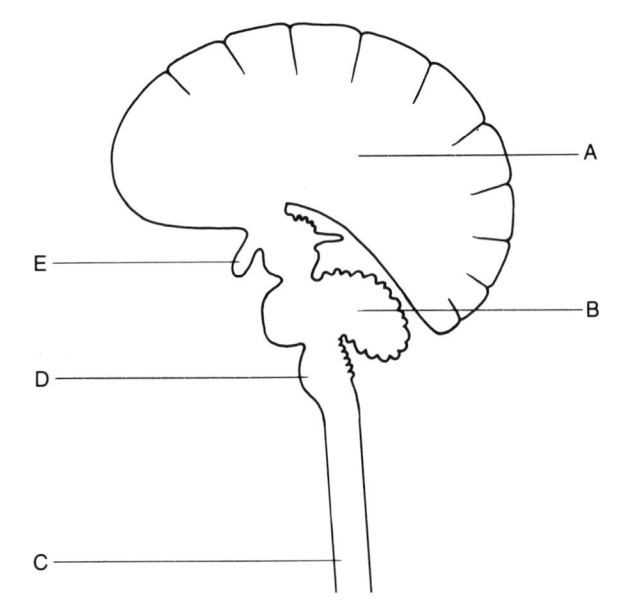

b) Replace the letters A–E with the correct labels chosen from the list below.

    cerebellum   cerebrum   medulla   pituitary gland   spinal cord

c) Which part of the brain is associated with each of the following functions?
   i) balance and muscle movements
   ii) intelligence and memory
   iii) control of breathing and beating of the heart

Did You Know?
Your brain uses up about 25 per cent of the oxygen you breathe in.

Topic 5 The body in action

19 Read this passage about heroin addiction and then answer the following questions:

Heroin was originally developed medically as a pain-killer, as a substitute for morphine, in the belief that it was less likely to produce addiction. The opposite has proved to be true. Heroin is one of the most addictive of all drugs. It is taken in various ways; it can be sniffed or smoked, but generally it is injected. In the early stages the needle is inserted just under the skin ('skin-popping'). The user will then progress to intravenous injection ('main-lining') by which stage he or she will have developed into an addict.

Immediately after a dose of heroin the user experiences a state of sleepy well-being called euphoria. This fades quickly, passing into anxiety, agitation and constant worry about getting the next dose. With habitual use a heroin addict normally goes through successive stages of physical, mental and moral deterioration. The way of life of an addict is characterised by personal neglect – irregular and insufficient meals, insanitary habits and a disregard for hygienic precautions during injections. Infections are common, e.g. abscesses and hepatitis. This neglect frequently leads to an early death, typically in the early thirties. The suicide rate among heroin addicts is said to be fifty times greater than it is in the general population. An addict who becomes pregnant may pass on the addiction to her baby. Immediate removal of the drug causes violent withdrawal symptoms which include sweating, convulsions, vomiting and diarrhoea. This is a painful and terrifying experience.

a) Why is it not desirable to use heroin medically as a pain-killer?

b) Briefly explain the following terms:

   addiction   euphoria   withdrawal symptoms

c) What is the difference between 'skin-popping' (line 5) and 'main-lining' (line 6)?

d) What is meant by 'physical, mental and moral deterioration' (line 11)?

e) What hygienic precautions should normally be taken before an injection?

f) What factors contribute to the early death of heroin addicts?

g) Why is withdrawal sickness known among addicts as 'the horrors'?

h) Addicts do not usually get pregnant because regular heroin injections tend to stop menstruation. Why might this be considered to be a fortunate effect?

4 Changing Levels of Performance

1 a) When do our muscles respire anaerobically?

b) Why can this not go on indefinitely?

c) Why do the following animals need to respire anaerobically for long periods of time?

i) tapeworms
ii) seals
iii) mud-burrowing worms

2 The heart rate of an athlete was recorded before, during and after a race for a total time of 100 minutes. The results are shown in the graph below.

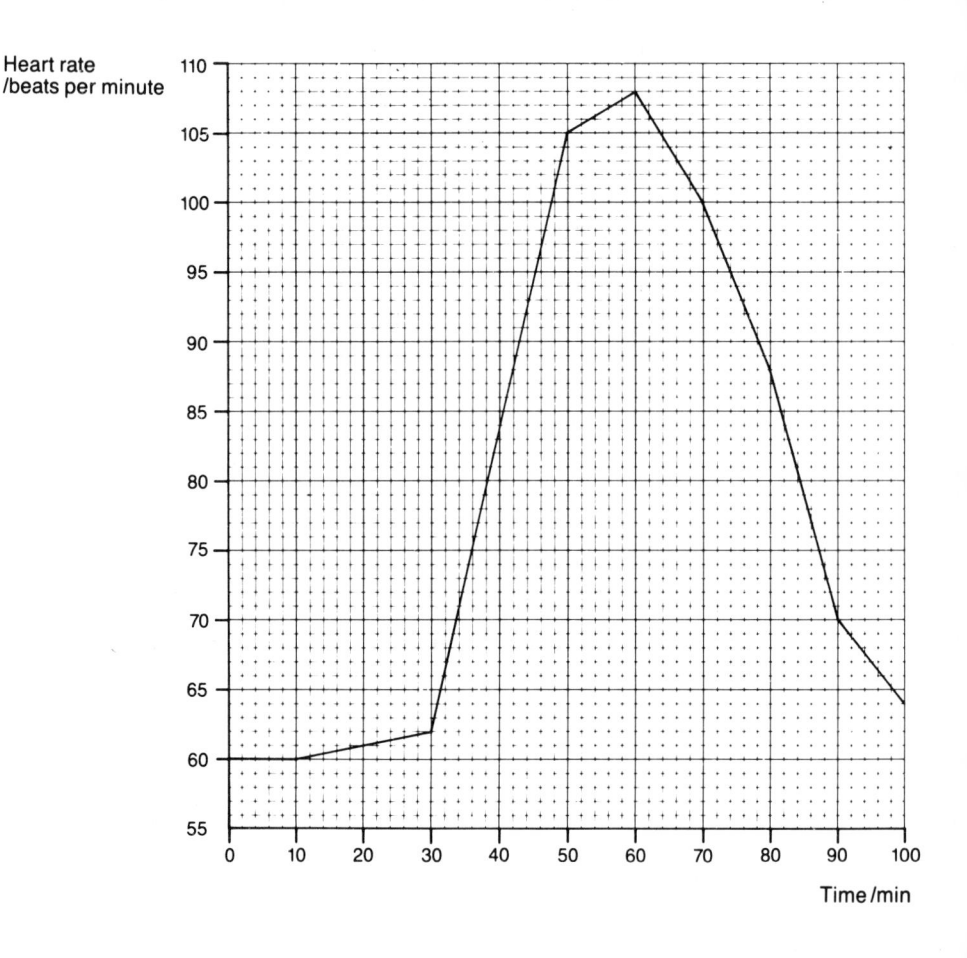

a) Using the information from the graph, complete the table of data below, showing the number of heartbeats at each of the time intervals.

Time /minutes	0	10	20	30	40	50	60	70	80	90	100
Heart rate /beats per minute											64

Topic 5 The body in action

b) What is the heart rate at rest?
c) After how many minutes did the athlete
   i) start the race?
   ii) stop running?
   Give a reason in each case.
d) Why did his heart rate increase just before he started running?
e) Give *two* reasons why the heart rate must increase during exercise.

3 Someone's heart rate was recorded at five-minute intervals. The results are given below.

Time /minutes	0	5	10	15	20	25	30	35	40	45	50	55	60	65	70	75	80	85	90	95	100	105
Heart rate /beats per minute	60	60	60	65	68	71	72	72	86	98	105	107	108	105	100	95	88	80	95	74	73	73

a) Plot a graph of these results. Label the axes as shown.

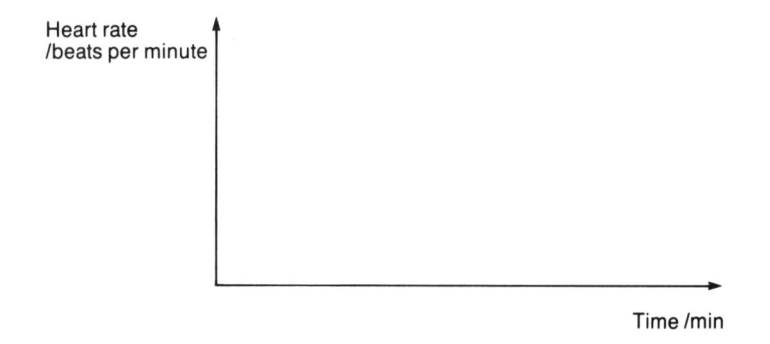

b) From the graph suggest the period of time when this person was
   i) frightened by a loud bang
   ii) sleeping
   iii) running
   iv) waking
c) Why does the heart rate need to increase when we are frightened?

4 Study the two graphs below, which show the effects of smoking on health.

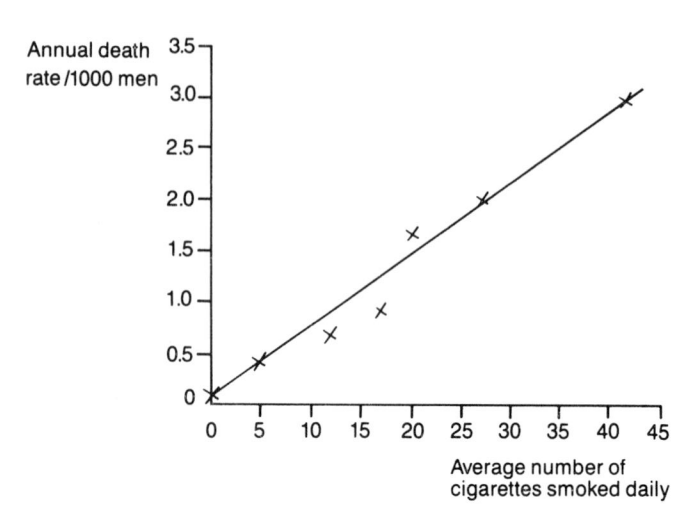

A Death rate from lung cancer among men smoking different numbers of cigarettes each day

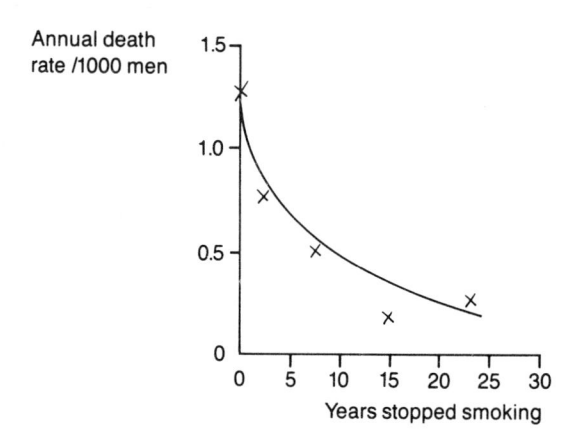

B Death rate from lung cancer among men who gave up smoking cigarettes

a) Out of a group of 5000 men smoking 30 cigarettes a day, how many are likely to die of lung cancer in one year?

b) What effect does giving up smoking have on a man's chance of contracting lung cancer?

Topic 6

Inheritance

1 Variation

1 Read the passage carefully then answer the questions that follow.

> The smallest group into which organisms are placed is a **species**. You would therefore expect members of the same species to be very similar. It is difficult to define how similar members of the same species must be, but the best definition is that **all members of the same species must be able to interbreed and produce offspring which can themselves reproduce.**
>
> A horse and a donkey are quite similar organisms and they can interbreed to produce a mule. However mules are sterile — they cannot themselves reproduce. Horses and donkeys belong to different species. They do however belong to the same genus — Equus. In zoos scientists have managed to breed lions and tigers together, but the offspring are sterile because lions and tigers belong to different species. All types of domestic dog are capable of interbreeding to produce mongrel puppies, which will eventually be capable of interbreeding with any other dog. Wolves look very similar to some dogs. However, wolves and dogs cannot interbreed.

a) Explain the following terms as they are used in the passage.
  i) interbreed
  ii) sterile
  iii) mule
  iv) genus

b) What must organisms be able to do to be classified as the same species?

c) Why can lions and tigers only interbreed in zoos?

d) Explain why
  i) all types of domestic dog belong to the same species.
  ii) wolves and domestic dogs belong to different species.

2 a) i) List *three* ways in which all humans are alike.
  ii) List *three* ways in which humans differ from one another.

b) Variation occurs in many other species of animals and plants,
  for example:

> number of petals on daisy flowers
> colour of tulip flowers
> height of oak-trees
> coat colour of labrador dogs.

Make a list of at least *six* further examples of variation found in animal and plant species.

Topic 6 Inheritance

3 a) This bar chart illustrates an example of **continuous variation**. Between the tallest and the shortest oak-tree there is a complete range of intermediates.

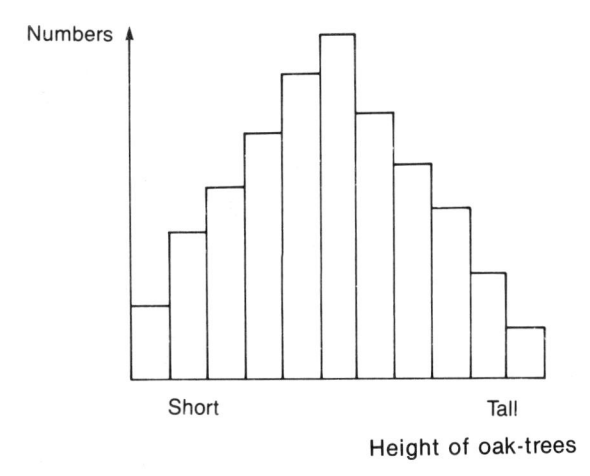

Height of oak-trees

i) Copy the bar chart.
ii) List *three* examples of continuous variation in humans.

b) This bar chart illustrates an example of **discontinuous variation**. The pea plants are either tall or dwarf. There are no 'in-betweens'.

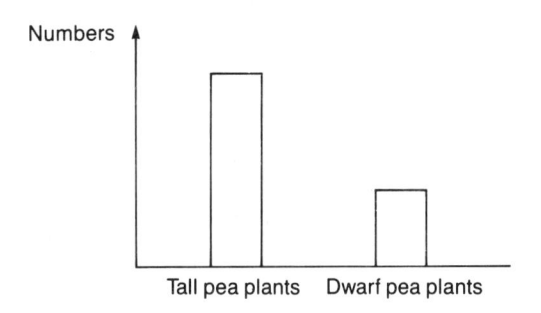

i) Copy the bar chart.
ii) List *three* examples of discontinuous variation in humans.

c) Explain the difference between continuous and discontinuous variation.

2 What is Inheritance?

1 Use the word 'inheritance' in a sentence which shows that you understand its meaning.

Topic 6 Inheritance

2 Read the passage below and then answer the following questions.

> Gregor Mendel carried out experiments with pea plants. In one experiment he studied how the height of the pea plant was inherited. He took *pure-breeding* tall plants and crossed them with *pure-breeding* dwarf plants. He collected the pea seeds that were produced and grew them to produce the F_1 generation. All the F_1 plants were tall.
>
> He then allowed the F_1 tall plants to self-fertilise. He collected the seeds and grew them to produce the F_2 generation. Three-quarters of these plants were tall, and one-quarter were dwarf.

a) Who was Gregor Mendel? When and where did he live?

b) If pure-breeding tall plants are self-fertilised what kind of plants will always grow from the seeds that are produced?

c) Which characteristic is dominant, tall or dwarf? How do you know this?

d) Did Mendel know about genes when he did his work?

e) How many genes that control the height of the plants are found in each cell of the pea plants?

f) How many genes for height are found in a pollen grain nucleus or egg cell?

g) Let the gene for tallness = T; let the gene for dwarfism = t. Complete this diagram to show the genes present in the gametes and F_1 plants.

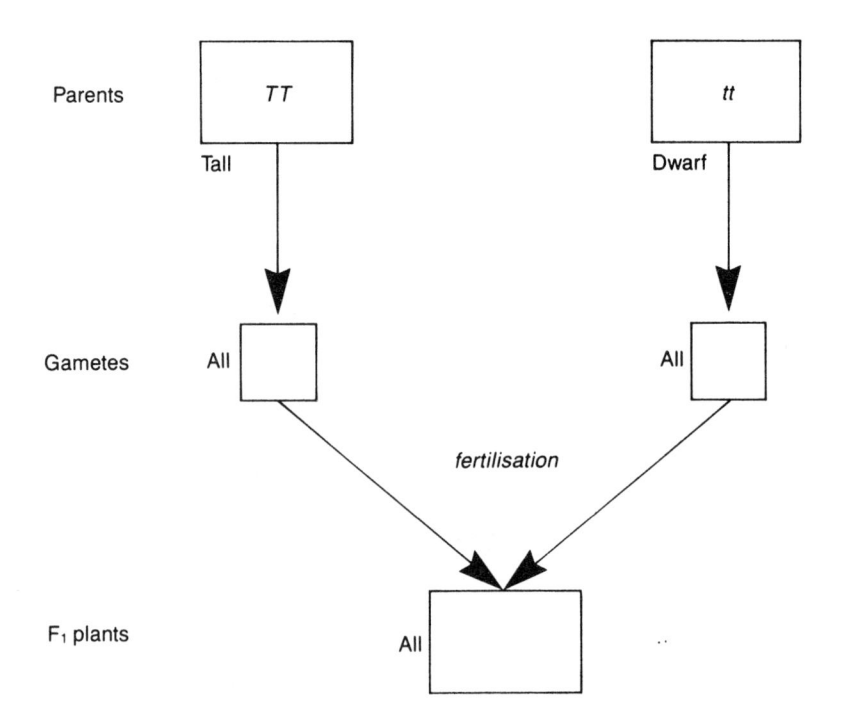

Parents: TT (Tall)   tt (Dwarf)

Gametes: All ☐   All ☐

fertilisation

F_1 plants: All ☐

Topic 6 Inheritance

h) Copy this diagram, which shows the cross between the F₁ plants and complete it by writing in the boxes the genes of the parents and the F₂ plants.

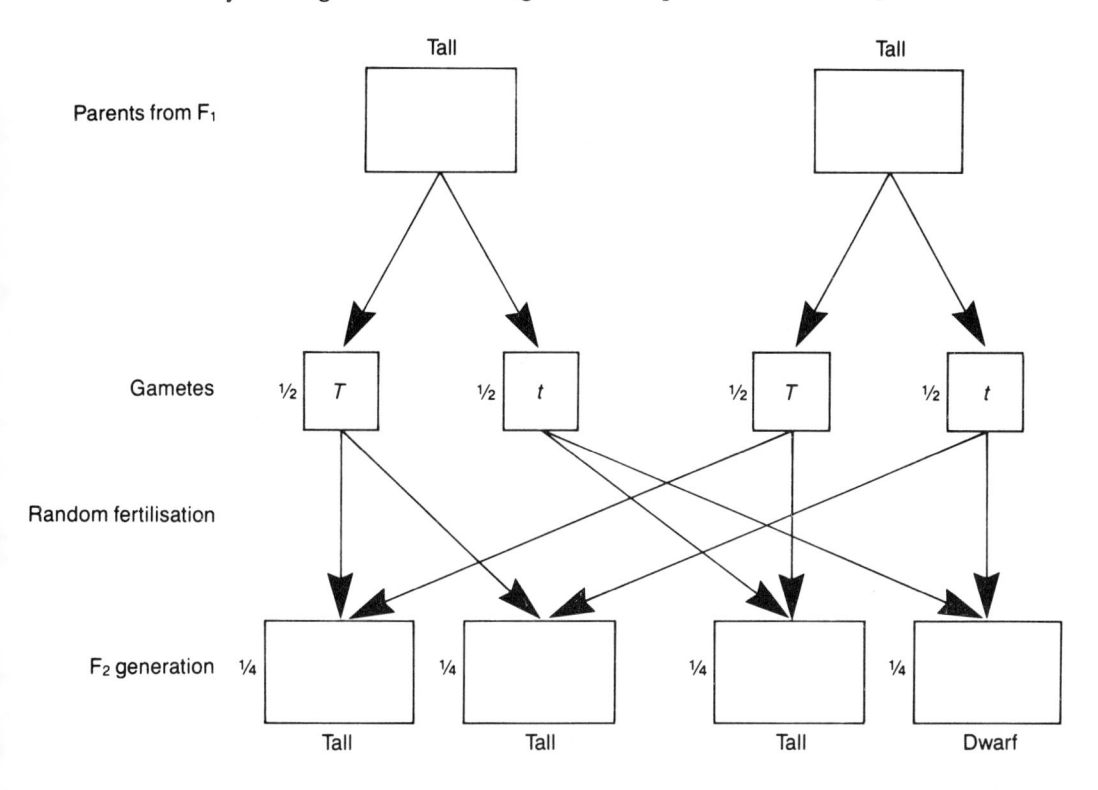

Parents from F₁ — Tall, Tall

Gametes: ½ T, ½ t, ½ T, ½ t

Random fertilisation

F₂ generation: ¼ Tall, ¼ Tall, ¼ Tall, ¼ Dwarf

i) Why is a capital letter used to represent the gene for tallness and a small letter used for the gene for dwarfism?

3 Match the words in the left-hand column with the definitions in the right-hand column.

Words	Definitions
phenotype	different forms of the gene for a particular characteristic
genotype	having two identical genes for a particular characteristic
pure breeding	a gene which can have its effects hidden
dominant	an organism's outward appearance
recessive	the genes that an organism contains
alleles	a gene which always produces an effect

4 Complete these sentences (a–d) by choosing the correct word from inside the brackets:

a) A pea plant whose (genotype/phenotype) is tall, could have the (genotype/phenotype) *TT* or *Tt*.

b) A tall pea plant with genotype *TT* is (homozygous/heterozygous) dominant.

c) A tall pea plant with genotype *Tt* is (homozygous/heterozygous) dominant.

d) A dwarf pea plant with genotype *tt* is (homozygous/heterozygous) recessive.

5 A gardener crossed 50 red-flowered tulips with 50 white-flowered tulips. The seeds of the cross germinated to produce only red-flowered tulips (F_1). The F_1 were self-fertilised and 1000 F_2 plants were obtained.

a) Which of the two colours is dominant?

b) If *R* is the symbol for the red gene and *r* is the symbol for the white gene, how would you represent the F_1 plants?

c) Draw a diagram to explain how the F_2 generation plants were produced from the self-fertilising of the F_1 plants.

d) About how many red-flowered tulips would you expect in the F_2 generation?

e) About how many white-flowered tulips would you expect in the F_2 generation?

f) If a heterozygous red tulip (*Rr*) and a homozygous red tulip (*RR*) were each crossed with the recessive (white) parent, what differences would you expect to find between the two sets of offspring? Draw diagrams to show the crosses.

6 In mice, the coat colour black is dominant over the coat colour brown. Let the gene for black coat = *B* and the gene for brown coat = *b*.

a) Explain with the help of a diagram, how two black mice could produce a brown offspring.

b) If you had a black mouse, how could you prove that it was carrying a gene for brown coat colour, i.e. that it was heterozygous *Bb*?

7 In humans, the ability to roll the tongue is caused by a dominant gene. Using *R* to represent the gene for rolling and *r* that for non-rolling, explain the possible offspring that can be produced when the parents are:

a) a roller and a non-roller

b) two non-rollers

c) two rollers

8 Certain organisms are particularly suitable for studies in inheritance. One example is the fruit fly, *Drosophila*.
What features make *Drosophila* a suitable organism for studying inheritance?

Topic 6 Inheritance 137

9 The diagram below shows the results of a cross between two fruit flies.

100 offspring were produced

Topic 6 Inheritance

There are four types of fruit fly in the diagram on the previous page.

Male long   Male short   Female long   Female short

a) Count the numbers of each type of fruit fly produced by the cross and record your results in a table.

b) Give suitable symbols for the two alleles for wing length — long and short.

c) Using these symbols give the **genotypes** of the parent fruit flies that produced these offspring.

10 Choose words from this list to fill in the gaps in the passage below:

  7   23   46   127   nucleus   genes   homologous
  divide   number   pairs   staining

Chromosomes are found in the _____ of every living cell. They can be seen by _____ a cell that is about to _____. For each thread-like chromosome there is another one exactly like it; therefore chromosomes occur in _____. Every body cell of a particular organism has the same _____ of chromosomes. For example, all humans have _____ chromosomes in each body cell, made up of _____ pairs. The cells of the garden pea have 14 chromosomes made up of _____ pairs and those of the shrimp have 254 chromosomes, made up of _____ pairs. The two chromosomes belonging to a matching pair are called _____ chromosomes.

11 This is a drawing of the chromosomes of a fruit fly.

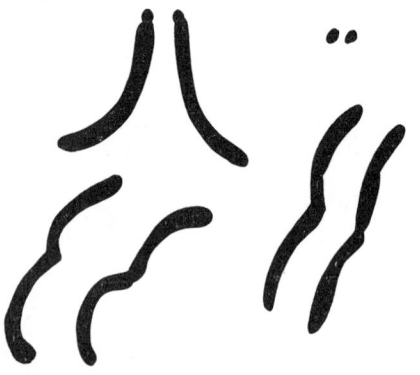

a) What is the chromosome number of this organism?

b) How many matching pairs are there?

12 a) If a human egg and a human sperm each carried 46 chromosomes, how many chromosomes would there be in the fertilised egg?

Topic 6   Inheritance

  b) How many chromosomes would there be in all the cells of the baby which grew from that fertilised egg?

  c) How many chromosomes must there be in human eggs and sperms to prevent the doubling of the chromosome number?

13 Meiosis is the special process of cell division that occurs in the formation of gametes.

  a) Copy and complete the diagram below by drawing in the nuclei of the four cells produced when the original cell divides by *meiosis*.

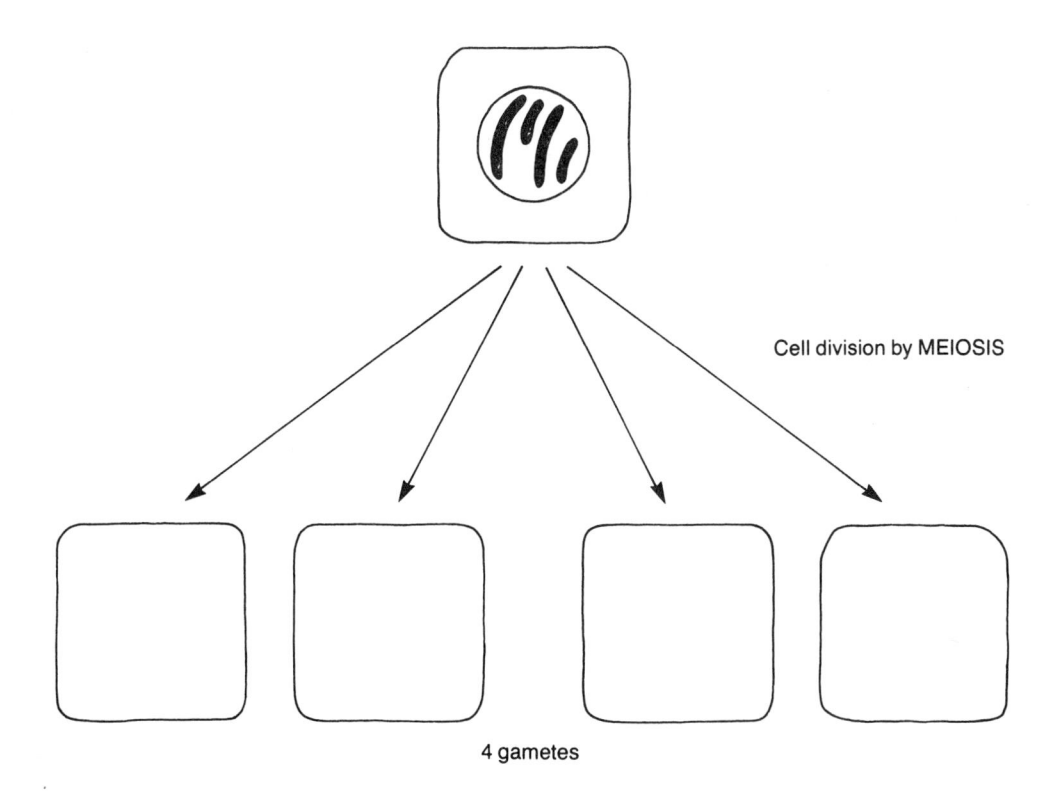

Cell division by MEIOSIS

4 gametes

  b) Why is meiosis also known as 'reduction division'?

  c) Where does meiosis occur in

    i)   a mammal?

    ii) a flowering plant?

  d) Explain why it is necessary for gametes to be formed in this way.

14 In this diagram of the human life cycle the circles represent the cells.

a) Copy and complete the diagram below by writing in the circles the numbers of chromosomes found in those cells.

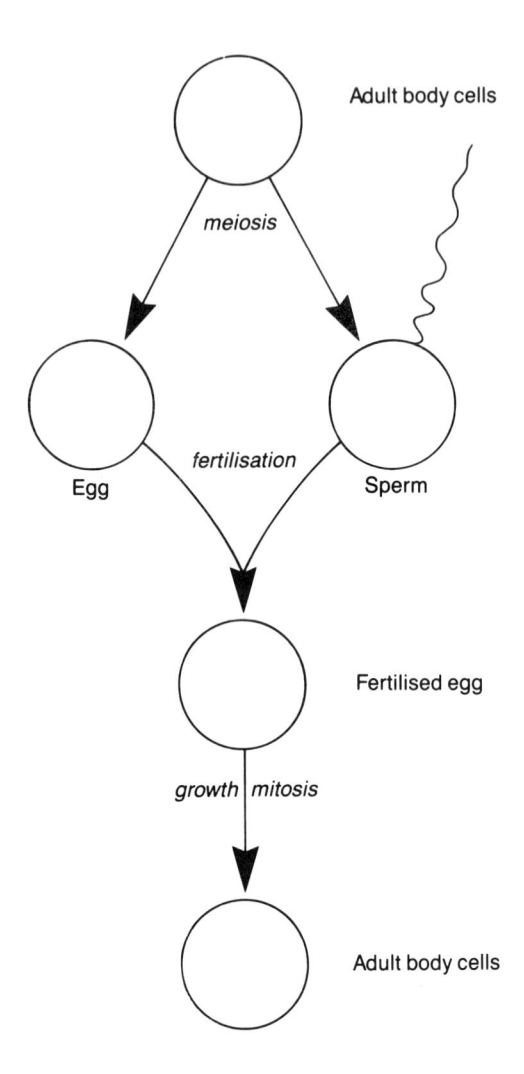

○ Adult body cells

meiosis

○ Egg   ○ Sperm

fertilisation

○ Fertilised egg

growth | mitosis

○ Adult body cells

b) Which of the cells in the diagram are **diploid** (have the full number of chromosomes) and which are **haploid** (have only half the full number)?

15 a) What are **sex chromosomes**?
b) How do human males and females differ in their sex chromosomes?
c) How many sex chromosomes are found in a gamete?

Topic 6 Inheritance

16 The diagram below shows the sex chromosomes of a human couple, Ada and Bill, four of their children (Cathy, Dora, Edward and Fred) and the gametes from which these children began.

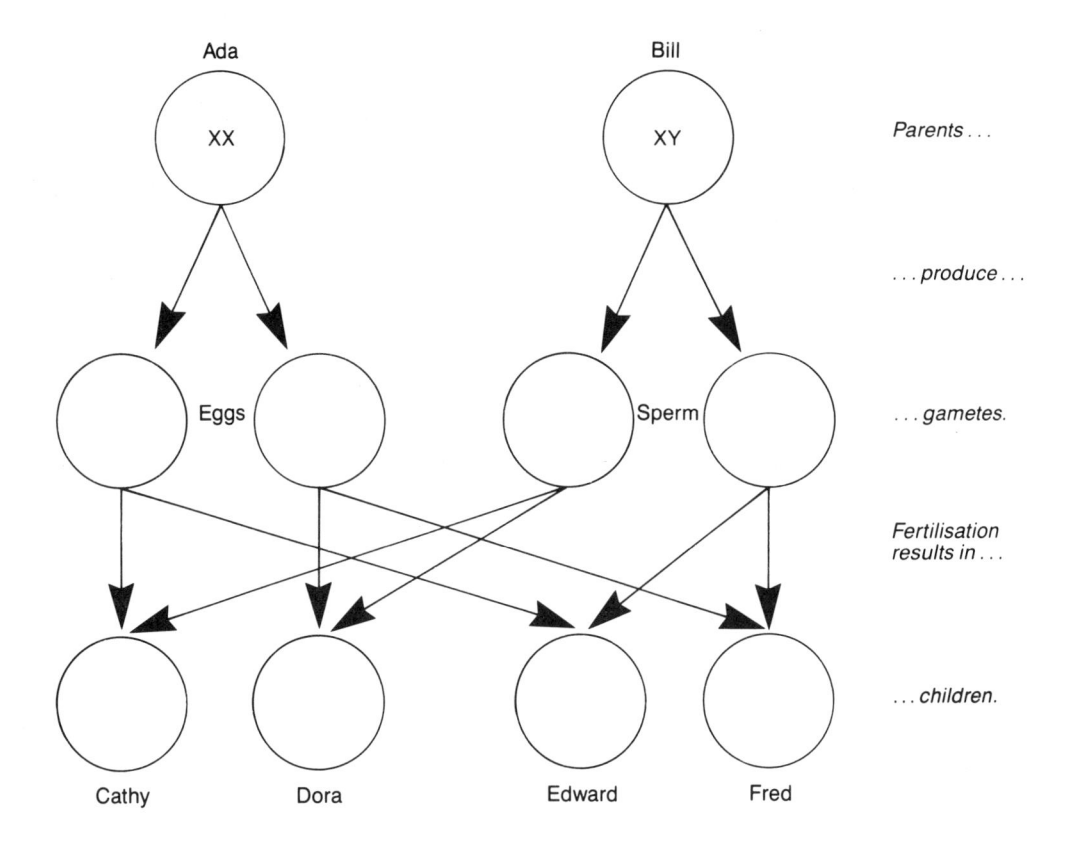

a) Copy the diagram and fill in the sex chromosomes of the gametes and children.
b) If another child was expected, what would be its chance of being a boy?
c) Name the type of cell division that produces gametes.

3 Genetics and Society

1 Read the passage (on the next page), which is about **selective breeding**, and answer the questions that follow.

Man has cultivated plants and kept animals for about 10 000 years. Over this time he has bred them selectively to produce desirable characteristics. For example, modern varieties of cattle have been bred over a very long time to give a high milk yield or fast meat production. From the varied individuals amongst a herd of cattle, breeders choose only those with desirable characteristics to breed and produce the next generation. Plant breeders have bred varieties of wheat and rice that grow more quickly, give a higher yield of grain and are more resistant to disease.

However the varieties of animals and plants that have been specially bred by man, would very often be unable to survive in the wild. Some farmers are now beginning to think differently about the characteristics they want in their animals and plants. Instead of enormous yields, they are now looking for varieties of crops that can grow well with less fertilisers or pesticides and varieties of animals that require less expensive housing and food. Luckily many of the older breeds that have these desirable characteristics have been conserved. These can be used in breeding programmes to develop new varieties.

a) What is meant by 'selective breeding'?

b) What are the advantages to man of breeding new varieties of food crops, such as wheat and rice?

c) According to the passage, what characteristics might be developed by plant and animal breeders in the future?

d) Why is it important to conserve the older varieties of animals and plants?

2 The diagrams opposite show the chromosomes of two different children.

a) Study the diagrams and give *two* differences between child A and child B.

b) Which child has an abnormal set of chromosomes?

c) What is the name of the genetic disorder caused by the abnormality?

d) How can chromosome defects be detected before birth?

3 Read this passage and answer the questions that follow it. The passage is about the **evolution** of bread wheat and is adapted from *The Ascent of Man by* J. Bronowski.

The turning point in the spread of agriculture was almost certainly the occurrence of two forms of wheat with large, full heads of seeds. Before 8 000 BC, wheat was not the luxuriant plant it is today; it was merely one of many wild grasses that spred throughout the Middle East. By some genetic accident, the wild wheat crossed with a natural goat grass and formed a fertile hybrid. The fourteen chromosomes of wild wheat were combined with the fourteen chromosomes of goat grass, and produced **Emmer** with twenty-eight chromosomes. The seeds of Emmer wheat were much plumper than the wild wheat and were attached to the husk in such a way that they scattered in the wind. For such a hybrid to be fertile is rare but not unique among plants.

Topic 6 Inheritance

Child A

1	2	3	4	5	6	X
7	8	9	10	11	12	
13	14	15	16	17	18	
19	20	21	22			Y

Child B

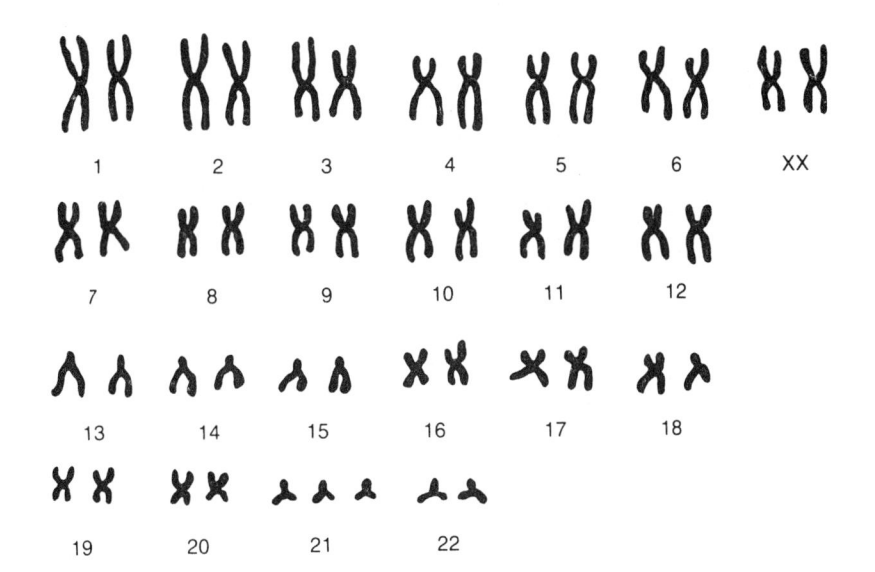

1	2	3	4	5	6	XX
7	8	9	10	11	12	
13	14	15	16	17	18	
19	20	21	22			

There was a second genetic accident in which Emmer crossed with another natural goat grass and produced a still larger hybrid with forty-two chromosomes, which is **bread wheat**. However this wheat can only be propagated by man. The seeds will never spread in the wind because the ear is too tight to break up. The life of each, man and plant, depends on the other. It is a true fairy tale of genetics — as if the coming of civilisation had been blessed in advance by the spirit of the abbot Gregor Mendel.

a) Why was the occurrence of wheat with large full heads of seeds a 'turning point' to the spread of agriculture?

b) Consider a plant with a chromosome number of fourteen.

   i) How many chromosomes would you normally expect to find in the gametes of this plant?

   ii) What would you expect to be the chromosome number of the offspring grown from a seed of this plant?

c) Why is the crossing of wild wheat with a natural goat grass described as a genetic accident?

d) What is a 'hybrid'?

e) Why would bread wheat not survive in the wild?

Topic 7

Biotechnology

Topic 7 Biotechnology

1 Living Factories

1 Below are some features of aerobic and anaerobic respiration. Construct a table with these two headings:

Aerobic respiration	Anaerobic respiration

Decide which feature belongs to which column, and then complete the table.

a) does not need oxygen

b) needs oxygen

c) releases a lot of energy

d) releases a little energy

e) produces ethanol and carbon dioxide in plants

f) produces lactic acid in animals

g) produces carbon dioxide and water in animals and plants

2 Use the library to find out more about one of the following:

a) The production of butter, cheese and yoghurt

b) Brewing

c) Bread-making

3 The diagrams at the top of the next page show the results of an experiment using yeast and sugar solutions carried out at a temperature of 20 °C.

a) Explain why the balloon has blown up in Tube D.

b) Explain why the balloons have not blown up in Tubes A, B and C.

c) Name *two* substances that would be produced in the test-tube containing yeast and sugar solution.

d) What would have been the result if dry yeast and sugar had been used instead of solutions? Explain your answer.

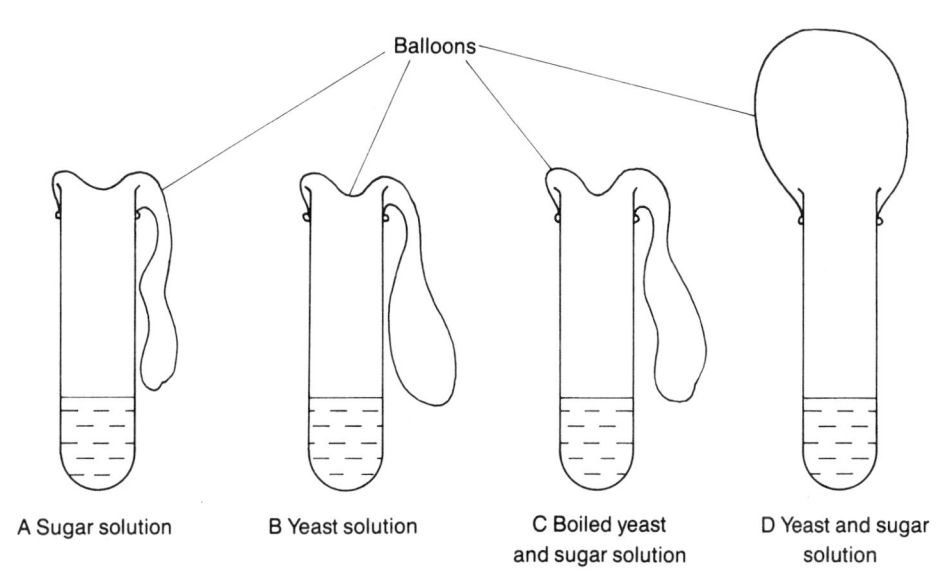

Topic 7 Biotechnology

Balloons

| A Sugar solution | B Yeast solution | C Boiled yeast and sugar solution | D Yeast and sugar solution |

e) What would you expect the results to be if the yeast and sugar solution had been kept at the following temperatures?

　i)　　0 °C

　ii)　 35 °C

　iii)　80 °C

4 A test-tube containing some yeast and sugar solution was placed in a water bath as shown in the diagram. After ten minutes the rate of bubbling was measured. The experiment was then repeated with the temperature of the water bath at each of the temperatures shown in the table on the next page.

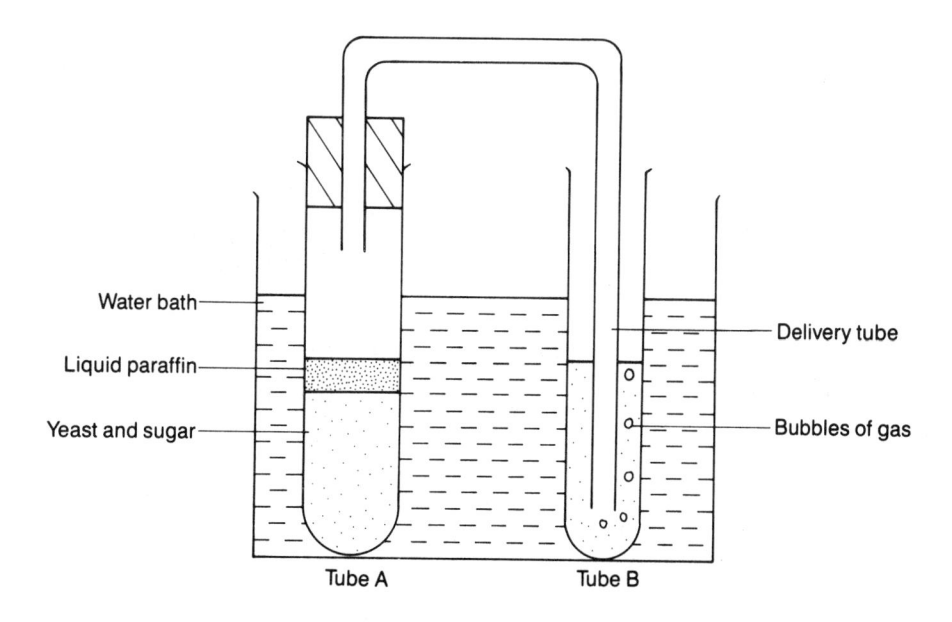

Water bath

Liquid paraffin

Yeast and sugar

Delivery tube

Bubbles of gas

Tube A　　　Tube B

Temperature /°C	10	20	30	40	50	60
Number of gas bubbles per minute	5	12	20	26	28	14

a) Plot a graph of the results, labelling the axes as shown.

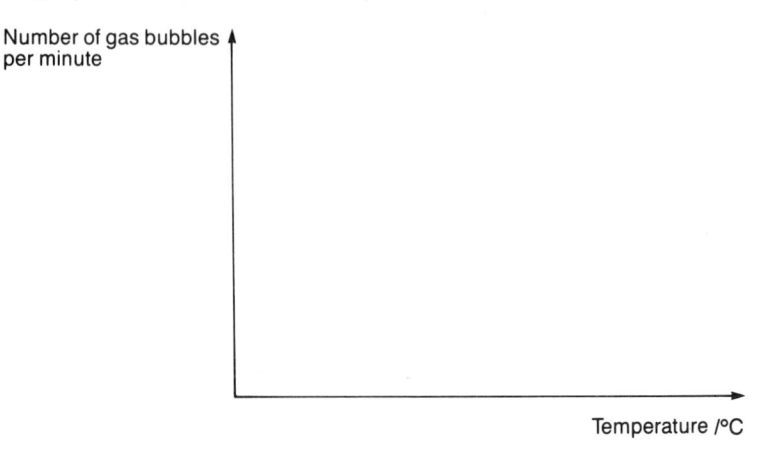

Number of gas bubbles per minute (y-axis)

Temperature /°C (x-axis)

b) What is the function of the liquid paraffin?

c) Give one reason why the apparatus was left for ten minutes at each temperature before any bubbles were counted?

d) Name the process taking place in the yeast cells, which produces the gas.

e) Name the gas being produced.

f) What substance could be used to identify this gas in Tube B?

g) Why did the number of bubbles decrease at 60 °C? (*Clue:* this process is controlled by enzymes.)

h) Give *two* reasons why the yeast cells would die in Tube A after about a week at 40 °C.

i) Write a simple equation to summarise what is happening in the above experiment.

j) What are *two* ways in which humans have taken advantage of this process?

2 Problems and Profit of Waste

1 Carefully read the passage on the next page about how we can grow bacteria, and then answer the questions.

Topic 7 Biotechnology

To grow bacteria they must be given moisture, warmth and plenty of food. Many years ago it was discovered that they will grow on the surface of a jelly-like material obtained from seaweed. This is called **agar**. Various food substances are added to the agar: this makes it an ideal **nutrient medium** in which to grow, or **culture**, bacteria.

The agar is usually put in a shallow **Petri dish**. This must be sterilised beforehand and kept covered, otherwise moulds may grow on the agar. To speed up their growth the bacteria should be kept warm: this is best achieved by putting the Petri dish in an **incubator**, a warm box in which the temperature can be kept constant.

Now suppose you put some bacteria on the surface of some nutrient agar. In the course of the next day or two the bacteria multiply into **colonies**. Each colony consists of thousands of bacteria clumped together. The individual bacteria are too small to be seen with the naked eye, but the colonies are clearly visible.

Bacterial colonies vary in size, shape and colour, according to the type of bacteria which give rise to them.

a) What conditions do bacteria need in order to grow?

b) What is agar?

c) What is added to agar to make it an 'ideal nutrient medium'?

d) Explain the meanings of the following words as used in the passage:

   culture   sterilised   colony   incubator

e) Why must the Petri dish and agar jelly be sterile?

f) How could they be sterilised?

g) Why should you wash your hands thoroughly before starting to culture bacteria in this way?

h) Explain carefully how you would 'put some bacteria on the surface of some nutrient agar'.

i) The agar plates are incubated at 35°C. Why?

j) The plates should be sealed before incubating them. Why?

k) Agar plates are usually incubated upside down. Can you think why?

l) Why must you wash your hands after handling the plates?

2 An experiment was set up as shown using tubes A–F as follows.

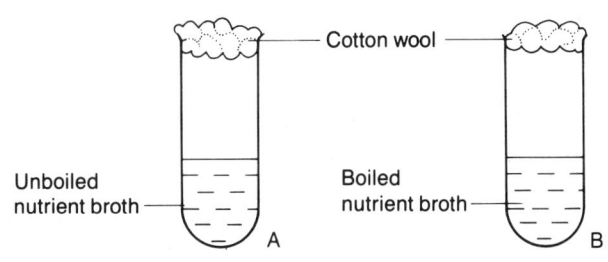

Diagram

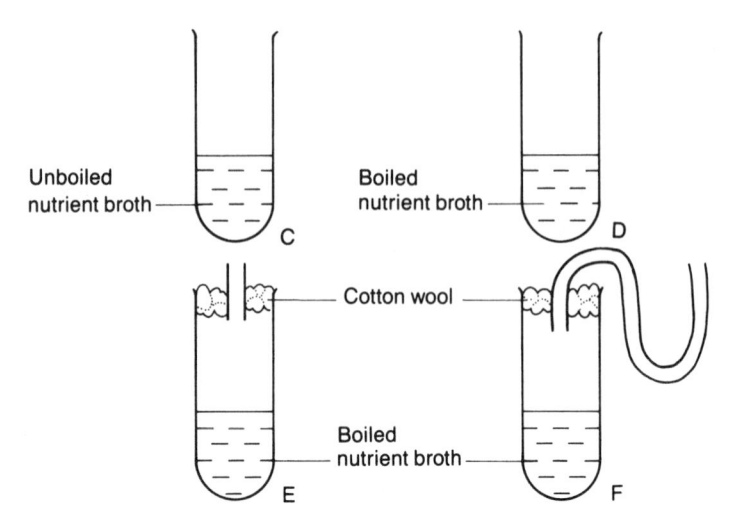

Tubes C (Unboiled nutrient broth) and E (Boiled nutrient broth) with cotton wool; tubes D (Boiled nutrient broth) and F (Boiled nutrient broth) connected via curved tube.

a) In which of the tubes would the broth go cloudy? Give reasons for your choices.

b) What difference would you expect in the results of tubes D and E? Why?

c) Explain the different results in tubes E and F.

3 There are living organisms in the soil which are too small to be seen with the naked eye or even a hand-lens.

a) Name *two* different groups of such organisms.

b) What do they feed on?

c) What benefit are these micro-organisms to larger plants growing in the soil?

d) Give a detailed account, with diagrams, of how you would set up an experiment to show that these micro-organisms are present in soil. Point out any controls you would need, and describe the results you would expect.

4 a) Choose words from the list below to complete the following sentences about **decay**.

    atmosphere   carbon dioxide   microbes   nitrogen   plants
    simpler   soil   water

i) Dead bodies are decayed by _____.

ii) During decay complex chemicals are broken down into _____ ones.

iii) Carbohydrates are broken down into _____ and _____.

iv) Proteins are broken down into _____ salts.

v) The simple substances can be absorbed and used by _____.

vi) The process of decay puts back into the _____ and _____ the chemicals that plants take out.

Topic 7 Biotechnology

b) i) Explain why manure and compost are good for plant growth.

ii) Why must fertiliser be applied to soil that has been used to grow crops?

5 a) Copy the diagram below which represents a sewage works.

b) Copy and complete the following table:

Part of sewage works	Description of the process that occurs there
A Sieve	
B Grit tank	Heavy particles such as grit sink to the bottom and can be removed.
C Settlement tank	
D Filter bed	
E Humus tank	The liquid leaving the filter beds contains dead plants and animals which lived among the stones in the filter bed. This is *humus*. In the humus tank the liquid is left undisturbed so that the humus settles to the bottom and the purified effluent can be separated and passed into a river.

c) Use the information in the table to label the parts A to E on your diagram.

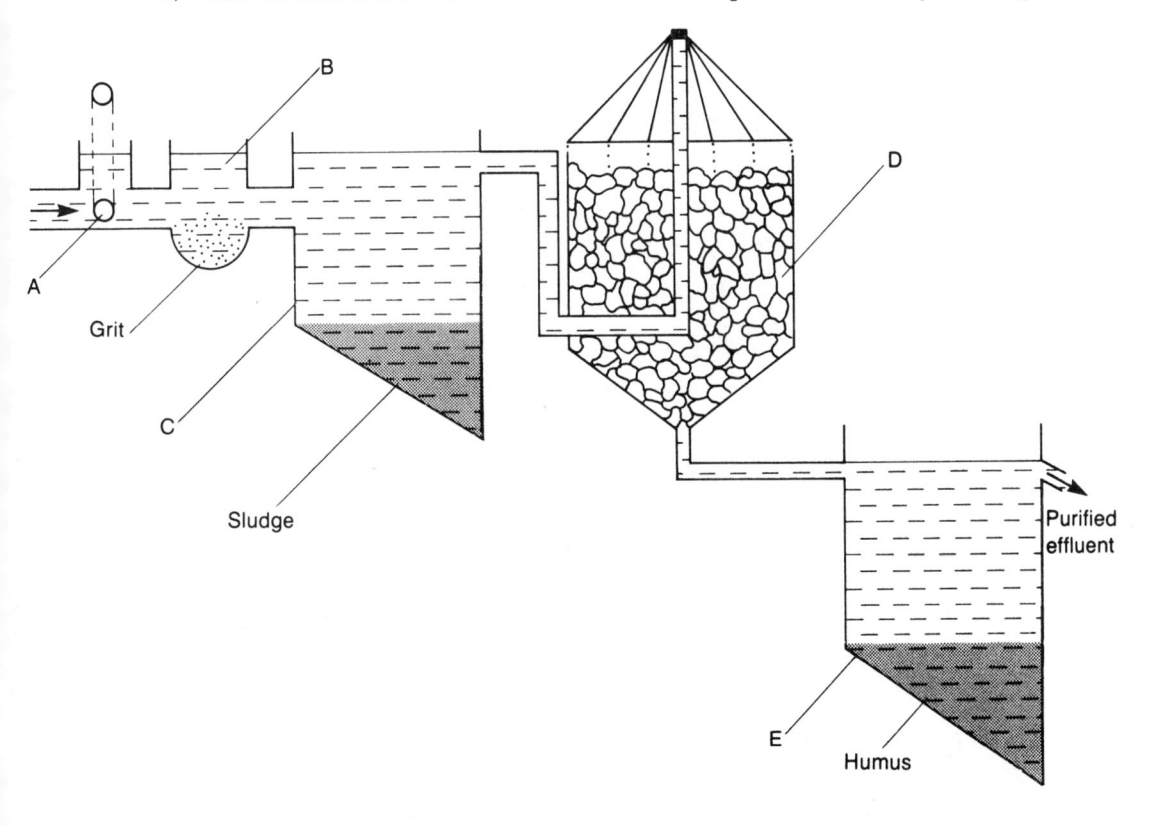

Topic 7 Biotechnology

d) What is sewage? Why is it dangerous to health?

e) How is the sewage carried to the sewage works?

f) Anaerobic bacteria feed on the sludge and produce a gas which can be used as a fuel to run the sewage works. When this process is complete, the sludge is dried.

   i) Name the gas produced.

   ii) What can the dried sludge be used for?

g) What other methods are used for the disposal of sewage?

6 Read this short passage about the production of **biogas**, then answer the following questions.

> When vegetable and animal matter rots in the absence of air, a gas is given off. The gas is usually about 60 per cent methane, the rest being mostly carbon dioxide. This biogas is a good fuel, particularly for cooking, heating and lighting in the home.
> Rubbish is often tipped into holes in the ground. This is called **landfill**. This rubbish will also generate biogas.

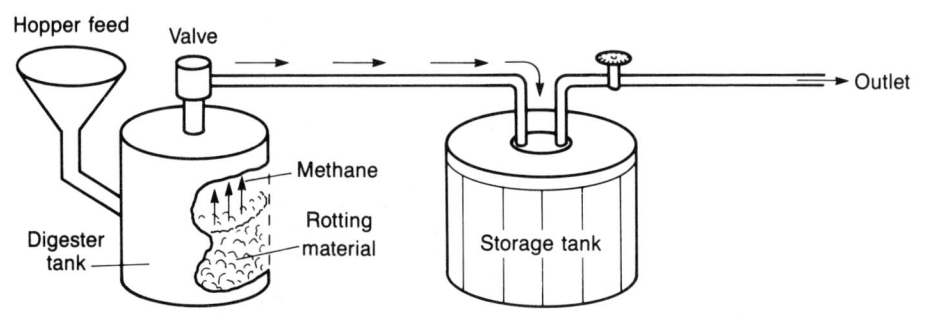

A biogas generator

a) Why is the gas called biogas?

b) Why is biogas particularly easy to make on farms?

c) What use can be made of the solid material left behind in the digester?

d) What type of organism is responsible for producing biogas from vegetable and animal matter?

e) Design and draw a suitable method for collecting biogas from a landfill site.

f) What kinds of household rubbish would work best at producing biogas?

Topic 7 Biotechnology

7 Read this passage, which is about the use of alcohol as a **fuel**, then answer the following questions.

> Sugar cane is a fast-growing tropical plant. The sugar it provides can be fermented to make alcohol. Alcohol can be used instead of petrol in cars. It is often mixed with petrol to produce **gasohol**.
> After the sugar cane has been crushed to remove the sugar, a woody material called **bagasse** is left. This can be used as a solid fuel to provide heat for the distillation of the fermented sugar.
> In Brazil many cars now run on alcohol fuel made this way and Brazil has plans to replace all petrol by alcohol.

a) By what process is the sun's energy converted into chemical energy in the sugar?

b) Explain the meaning of the words 'fermented' and 'distillation'.

c) What is
   i) gasohol?
   ii) bagasse?

d) Why is it particularly advantageous for Brazil to produce fuel in this way?

e) How is this process an example of biotechnology?

f) To grow enough sugar cane to replace all liquid fuels with alcohol, Brazil would have to create new farmland by clearing parts of the Amazon jungle. What problems would this cause?

8 Read the passage which is about energy from biomass and answer the following questions (a–g).

> With fossil fuels running out, the world needs renewable energy sources that can be re-made as fast as they are used up. Plant material (biomass) is a good renewable energy source.
> Biomass energy is particularly important in developing countries, which often do not have their own fossil fuels and cannot afford to buy them. Examples of biomass fuels are wood, charcoal, alcohol, vegetable oil and biogas (methane).
> A tenth of the energy stored by the process of photosynthesis could provide all the world's energy needs.

a) What is the ultimate source of energy in the world?

b) What is a fossil fuel? Give an example.

c) What is a renewable energy source?

d) What is biomass?

e) Give *four* examples of biomass fuels.

f) Why is biomass energy particularly important in developing countries?

g) Why are tropical countries generally better able to produce biomass fuels than cool countries like Britain?

9 A single bacterium is capable of dividing once every 20 minutes in 'good' conditions.

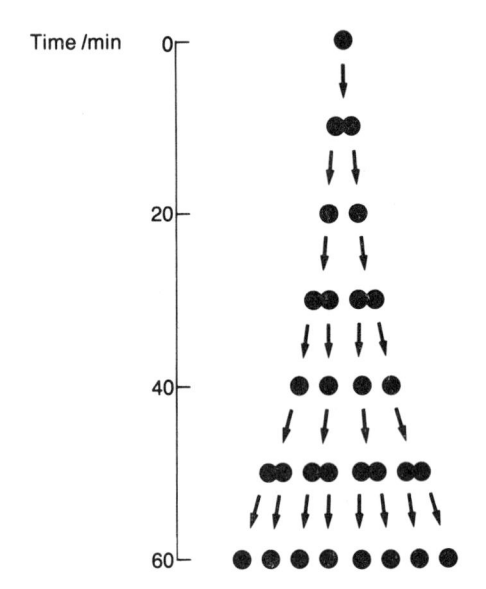

a) What would be 'good' conditions for bacteria to grow in?

b) Starting with a single bacterium, how many bacteria would there be after

  i) one hour?

  ii) two hours?

  iii) three hours?

10 Read this passage which is about micro-organisms as food for humans and answer the following questions.

> Bacteria can be grown to make a protein-rich food called single-cell protein (SCP). A variety of substances can be used by the bacteria to produce SCP. These include natural gas, methanol, manure and food wastes such as citrus peel and milk whey. SCP is an excellent protein which can be produced quickly, in vast quantities. Its production uses little space and it can be easily stored as a powder. It is used at present as an animal feed for chickens and calves, but could be used for human consumption.

Topic 7 Biotechnology

Mycoprotein is a fungus. It contains about 45 per cent protein and is high in fibre. It can be used to make artificial meat by adding appropriate flavourings. It has a texture which is chewy and similar to meat.

a) What organisms are used to make SCP?

b) Name one food waste used as a food base for SCP production.

c) Give *three* advantages of SCP.

d) Why do you think it is used only as animal food at the moment?

e) What is mycoprotein?

f) Why is mycoprotein more suitable than SCP for human consumption?

11 Study the bar chart which compares the nutrients in mycoprotein and in beef, and answer the following questions.

a) Give three reasons why mycoprotein is a healthier food than beef. Explain your reasons.

b) Give two reasons why it would be better to eat beef than mycoprotein.

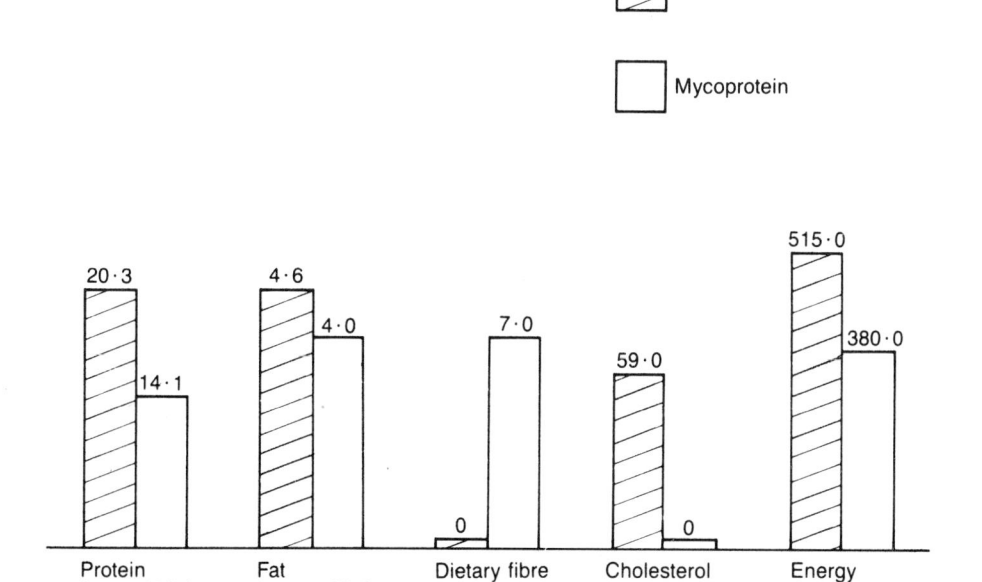

Bar chart key: Beef / Mycoprotein

- Protein (g per 100g): Beef 20.3, Mycoprotein 14.1
- Fat (g per 100g): Beef 4.6, Mycoprotein 4.0
- Dietary fibre (g per 100g): Beef 0, Mycoprotein 7.0
- Cholesterol (mg per 100g): Beef 59.0, Mycoprotein 0
- Energy (kJ per 100g): Beef 515.0, Mycoprotein 380.0

12

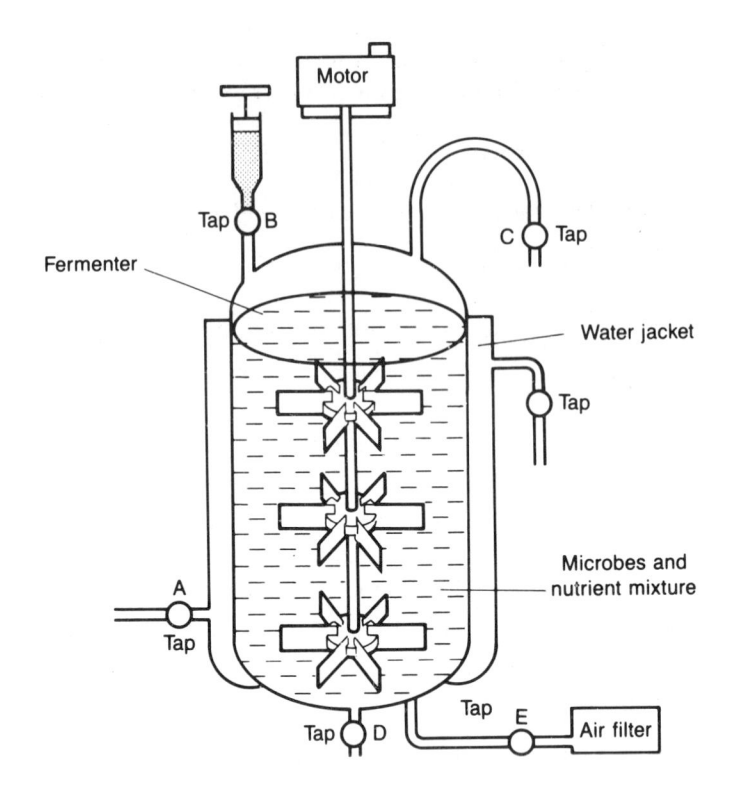

The diagram above shows an industrial fermenter. These are large containers in which microbes can be grown. There are many pipes and the taps are used to control the entry and exit of different substances.

a) Copy the above diagram.

b) Match the taps labelled A–E in the left-hand column with their correct functions in the right-hand column.

Taps   Function
A   adding nutrients to the mixture
B   adding air to the mixture
C   allowing waste gases to escape
D   draining off the products
E   pumping cold water into the water jacket

c) What is the function of
   i) the motor?
   ii) the air filter?

d) Why is cold water needed in the water jacket?

e) When empty, the fermenter is pumped through with steam. What is the reason for this?

Topic 7 Biotechnology

f) The fermenter can be used to produce mycoprotein. To do so, certain substances and conditions are needed. Copy and complete this table.

Substance or condition needed	Reason
Oxygen	
Sugar	
Ammonia	
Constant temperature of 32°C	

3 Reprogramming Microbes

1 Read this passage which is about **genetic engineering** and then answer questions (a–f).

Genetic engineering uses techniques that allow scientists to transfer genes from one organism to another. Simple, rapidly reproducing organisms like bacteria can be used as chemical factories for making substances needed by other organisms, such as humans. An example is insulin.

Many people suffer from a disease called diabetes, which means that they cannot make the hormone insulin. In healthy people it is produced after a meal and instructs the tissues to absorb glucose from the blood. Many diabetics inject insulin, taken from the pancreas of animals, into their bodies to replace the insulin they cannot make themselves. However, animal insulin differs slightly from the human variety and sometimes has unpleasant side effects.

Scientists now use genetic engineering to produce human insulin. They can transfer the insulin gene from human cells to a bacterium by using special enzymes. The bacterium reproduces rapidly, soon producing millions of bacterial cells, all able to make human insulin. Bacteria can be grown in huge numbers in large vats like those used for brewing beer. Therefore in the future the use of human insulin produced by bacteria should be common.

Another disease, that some people have, stops them from producing growth hormone in their pituitary glands. Unfortunately only human growth hormone can be used to treat these people. Until recently this could only be obtained from pituitary glands taken from corpses. Very large numbers of pituitary glands are needed to treat one individual. Genetic engineering techniques have now been developed that enable human growth hormone to be produced by bacteria.

a) Which organ of the body produces insulin?
b) What is the effect on the body of a deficiency of insulin?

Topic 7 Biotechnology

   c) Why is insulin from animals not as desirable for treating diabetics as human insulin?

   d) Why is it significant that bacteria
      i) reproduce very rapidly?
      ii) can be grown in huge numbers in large vats?

   e) What is the effect on the body of a deficiency of growth hormone?

   f) Explain how genetic engineering could be used to produce human growth hormone.

2 a) The table below gives some uses of enzymes. Copy and complete it.

Use	Enzyme involved	Explanation
Washing clothes	Proteases	Biological washing powders dissolve protein stains, e.g. blood.
Tenderising meat	Proteases	
Making syrup and fruit juice		Starch is broken down into sweet sugars.
	Cellulase	The tough cellulose cell walls are broken down.
Cheese-making	Rennin	

   b) The biological action of washing powder is reduced if the temperature of the wash is too high. Explain this.

3 Read the following passage carefully and then answer the questions.

      In 1866 Louis Pasteur was asked to investigate a mysterious disease that was killing off silk-worms in France and bringing ruin to farmers.
      Pasteur already knew about microbes and he suspected that they might be the cause of the disease. So he carried out the following experiment. He took a healthy silk-moth, killed it and crushed up the body. He looked at it under a microscope and could see only the cells of the moth. He then took a diseased moth, crushed it and looked at it under the microscope. He saw bacteria mixed with the cells of the moth.

   a) Why was it important for the silk farmers to find the cause of the disease?
   b) Why did they ask Louis Pasteur to help them?
   c) What did Pasteur suspect was the cause of the disease?

Topic 7   Biotechnology

d) What difference did Pasteur find between the healthy and the diseased moths?

e) Did Pasteur prove that the bacteria were the cause of the disease? If not, what further experiments might he have done?

4 Read the two passages a) and b) and answer the questions on each passage.

a) In 1928 Professor Alexander Fleming discovered that a mould found growing on a bacterial plate produced a substance that killed the bacteria on the plate. He went on to find out that this substance produced by the mould had the power of destroying all kinds of bacteria that cause human disease. He identified the mould as *Penicillium notatum*.

Fleming injected this bacteriocidal substance into mice and found that it did them no harm. However he also found that the substance lost its power to kill bacteria if kept for any length of time.

i) Explain the following:

   mould   bacterial plate   bacteriocidal

ii) What name was given to the substance produced by the mould?

b) Surprisingly, there was very little interest in Fleming's discovery. It was not until 1938 that two scientists from Oxford called Florey and Chain repeated Fleming's experiments. They obtained the same results and also showed that the substance could kill harmful bacteria that had been injected into mice.

Most of their tests were completed by 1940, and because it was now wartime there was an urgent need for such a drug. Many scientists worked to find a way of making and preserving it in a new pure form. Eventually they succeeded and it began to be made commercially.

i) Why is it surprising that there was no interest in Fleming's discovery for ten years?

ii) How might Florey and Chain have shown that 'the substance could kill harmful bacteria that had been injected into mice'.

iii) Why was there an urgent need in wartime for a drug with the power to kill bacteria?

iv) What name is given to all substances that are produced by microbes and have the power to kill bacteria?

v) Name *two* diseases that can now be easily cured by these drugs but would probably have caused death 60 years ago.

5 Substance X is extracted from a living organism. The diagram on the next page shows the effect it has on bacteria growing on agar jelly. Disc A has been soaked in a high concentration of X; disc B has been soaked in a low concentration of X; disc C was soaked in distilled water only. The three discs were placed on the surface of the agar jelly using sterile forceps. Bacteria had already been introduced into the agar jelly. The agar plate with the three discs in position was incubated for eighteen hours at 37 °C.

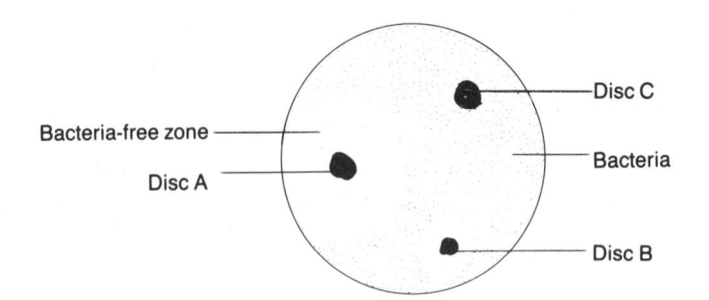

a) Why was disc C included in the experiment?
b) What effect does X appear to have on bacterial growth?
c) By what process would substance X get into the agar?
d) What is the general name given to a substance such as X?
e) Name one specific example of a substance that has properties similar to X's.

6 Choose words from this list to complete the following sentences:

milk   bread   penicillin   microbes   antibiotics   yeast
decay   protein   bacteria   vinegar   biotechnology

a) The use of microbes in industrial processes is known as _____.
b) Bacteria and fungi play a very important part in making dead organisms _____.
c) The process of sewage treatment depends on decay _____.
d) Butter, yoghurt, and cheese are made by the action of bacteria on _____.
e) The flavour of different cheeses is due to the action of different _____.
f) _____ is used to produce alcohol and to make _____ rise.
g) In the production of _____, bacteria are used to convert ethanol to acetic acid.
h) Bacteria and fungi can now be grown in special chambers to produce _____ as food for humans and animals.
i) Some microbes produce substances that can kill other microbes and prevent them from multiplying. These substances are called _____. An example of one is _____.